WORKPLACE BULLYING

By

Shelley Boulet

FriesenPress
One Printers Way
Altona, MB R0G0B0,
Canada

www.friesenpress.com

Copyright © 2021 by Shelley Boulet
First Edition — 2021

Editor: Laura Matheson

All rights reserved.

No part of this publication may be reproduced in any form, or by any means, electronic or mechanical, including photocopying, recording, or any information browsing, storage, or retrieval system, without permission in writing from FriesenPress.

ISBN
978-1-03-910139-5 (Hardcover)
978-1-03-910138-8 (Paperback)
978-1-03-910140-1 (eBook)

1. BUSINESS & ECONOMICS, EDUCATION

Distributed to the trade by The Ingram Book Company

Endorsements

"There are many books on the topic of unhealthy workplace cultures—and the associated behaviours that go along with them—so how is this book different? Well, Shelley has *lived (and survived)* working in unhealthy and psychologically unsafe workplaces. Rather than letting it destroy her, she has chosen to *shine light on dark places*, chosen *resilience*—'to be better, not bitter,' and taken what has happened and is using it as a *force for good*, not only as it relates to workplace relationships and interactions, but anytime we deal with human beings."

--Kari, Mediator, Facilitator, and Professional Investigator

"This is an excellent resource for all professionals, groups and individuals seeking to fully understand workplace bullying. Prevention, intervention, and repair or recovery options are included along with resources to further assist. Breaking the silence, talking about it, healing shame and self-doubt, and understanding those microaggressions as well as subtle nuances, are essential to creating long term sustainable changes in life, and in the workplace. There are many books, research papers, and services today, however, many lack defining the 'human experience of this abuse'. This author has done her homework both personally and professionally. I highly recommend this resource."

--Linda Crockett MSW, RSW, SEP, CCPA

https://instituteofworkplacebullyingresources.ca/

"I am grateful for Shelley taking the time to put pen to paper for all of our good. Her clear and thoughtful explanation of what really goes on in the workplace, helped me understand that I was not alone. Workplace bullying is real, happens at all levels and shockingly happens in those institutions which most people think are safe. Maybe therein lies the problem – when bully's feel safe they thrive and are able to practice their craft and create a toxic and inhumane environment. Shelley knows of what she speaks, has done the work and taken in upon herself to help everyone. As a business owner or elected official please take a look at your charge after reading Shelley's explanation of all the symptoms and causes of workplace bullying, be brave like Shelley and take those bullies to task! I draw your attention to the lengthy research done on Non-Disclosure Agreements a true identifier of toxic work environments. Permit people who demonstrate 'competence with a conscience' and not just competence to thrive, you will benefit from lower turnover, greater attendance, lower sick time and lower legal costs. Our people are the only asset that counts, we all know it and we all need to act like it. Shelley has turned an awful experience in to a useful tool for each of us to consider – she should be *commended* for standing up and sharing it and its lessons with us."

--Ross Robinson

Table of Contents

Acknowledgements	xi
The Emergence of "Workplace Bullying: The Pandemic Within"	xiii
Section 1	1
Chapter 1: Workplace Bullying & Harassment	3
Harassment	5
Bullying	6
Chapter 2: DARVO	13
Deny	14
Attack	15
Reverse Victim and Offender	16
Chapter 3: Human Rights in Canada	17
Chapter 4: Schoolyard vs. Workplace Bullies	21
Chapter 5: "Top 25 Tactics Adopted by all Bullies"	25
Chapter 6: Signs of Bullying in the Workplace	29
Chapter 7: Case Study – One of my Experiences Being Bullied	35
Section 2	63
Chapter 8: The Role of Corporate Culture in Workplace Bullying & Harassment	65
Chapter 9: Ignored Behaviour is Condoned Behaviour	69

Chapter 10: Leadership Styles 75

Autocratic 75

Bureaucratic 76

Democratic 77

Delegative 78

Strategic 79

Coaching 79

Visionary 80

Servant 81

Chapter 11: Examples of Poor Leadership 83

1. Assuming the Sick Aren't Sick 83

2. Requesting a Functional Abilities Form and Then Not Following It 85

3. Failing to Follow Policies 87

4. Avoiding/Ignoring/Discounting Glaring Leadership Issues 89

5. Tagging Employees 93

6. Leaders Advising Employees to Provide Negative Feedback on a Co-worker 96

7. Constructive Dismissal 100

8. Negligent Hiring and/or Retention 100

9. Conducting Reference Checks Without Consent	104
10. Gossip and Exclusion of Potential Candidates	105
11. HR Leaders Indicate Lack of Opportunities	106
12. Retaliation	108
13. Poorly Conducted / Sham Workplace Investigations	110
14. Lack of Confidentiality	111
15. Defamation of Previous Employee	112
16. Refusing to Provide Reference / Providing Negative Reference	113
17. Improper Use of Progressive Discipline	114
Chapter 12: Bullying and Harassment Cases	117
Other Canadian Cases of Interest	133
International Cases of Note	138
Chapter 13: Case Study – My Experience with the Peter Principle	141
Chapter 14: Progressive Discipline	143
Typical Steps of Progressive Discipline	145
Step 1: Verbal Warning	147
Step 2: Written Warning	149
Step 3: Suspension, Demotion, or PIP	149
Step 4: Termination	151
Exceptions	152

Chapter 15: Non-Disclosure Agreements 155

Chapter 16: Constructive Dismissal 159

Chapter 17: Working Toward Organizational Change 161

Section 3 163

Chapter 18: Bullying Investigations in the Workplace 165

The Elgert v Home Hardware Investigation 166

Elements of an Effective Workplace Investigation 167

Section 4 169

Appendix 175

Don't Rush to Judge Employees on Medical, Disability Leave 177

Addressing the Bystander Effect in the Workplace 181

Workplace Bullying: The Other Epidemic 185

What Can an Employer Do? 189

A Quick Guide for Conducting Workplace Investigations 191

Time's Up for Toxic Workplaces 197

Human Rights Tribunals 199

References 201

Acknowledgements

Thanks to Linda Crockett for the very fitting adjective "insidious" regarding bullying, your knowledge, and persistence in bringing ongoing awareness to workplace bullying and harassment.

Thank you, Jennifer Freyd, for your permission to include your descriptive quote!

Thank you, Dr. Gary Namie, for permission to include your article "Top 25 tactics adopted by all bullies"! It is very enlightening and relatable.

As a result of my insatiable desire to understand the issue of bullying and harassment, there were a number of avenues from which I greatly benefited and learned immensely. Besides reading resources provided by my counsellor, I searched and devoured all I could to learn and better understand. Connecting with numerous others experiencing similar situations provided further insight. And speaking to Linda Crockett at abrc.ca on more than one occasion helped me understand and comprehend far more than I can begin to state. I am immensely grateful to my counsellor, others targeted, literature, and various experts (Dr. Namie and Linda Crockett, to name a few).

Many thanks to Heather Ikin for her permission to include her article titled "The bystander effect."

My sincere appreciation to the Canadian Centre for Occupational Health and Safety (CCOHS), for their permission to include their article "What can an employer do?"

Thanks to Trenton. Your words of wisdom, experience of bullying, and further topics were helpful.

Your tactful words of wisdom are appreciated, Kari!

Ross and Jacquie, for your support and words of encouragement.

Stuart Rudnar, I am very appreciative to be able to include your invaluable article, titled "Don't Rush to Judge Employees on Medical, Disability Leave."

The editor of this book, for pushing me past my comfort zone. Initially, I was intent on saying little about my experience(s). They were still raw and painful to think about, let alone share. And, with so many other stories that are just as bad, and worse, instead of what looked more like a textbook, this book developed into what it is.

The cartoon by Cathy Wilcox, simply, yet eloquently captures the prevalent issues of toxic culture(s) within and workplace bullying. I am grateful for her permission to include it in section two.

All the people I have missed. I know there are several. I am fortunate to have had the support I do. For that, I am very thankful.

The Emergence of "Workplace Bullying: The Pandemic Within"

While I have been working on this book, the coronavirus (aka COVID-19) pandemic is ongoing. There are daily updates on numbers infected throughout the world, including deaths, those in hospital (along with those in intensive care), and recoveries.

Businesses are closed. While some closures are temporary, others result in permanent closures. There are employees working from home. While some workers have been laid off, there are others who have permanently lost their jobs. Some people who are unable to work are eligible for financial relief of some sort, while others are not.

Similar to people's varied perceptions of coronavirus/COVID-19, there are numerous and varied perceptions on harassment/bullying, including whether it actually exists. And much like the coronavirus/COVID-19, there are a lot of misunderstandings about workplace bullying/harassment. There are believers and non-believers, misunderstandings over the differences between school bullies and workplace bullies, disagreements about tactics/methods employed by bullies, and debates about what constitutes bullying.

Added to this are the degree of bullying experienced, how to address/deal with situations adequately, who should/shouldn't address bullying, how to effectively handle each situation, who can/cannot deal with situations (including investigations), and so on.

Those personally experiencing harassment within organizations of any kind are painfully aware not only of the experience, but also of its after-effects. Virtually every and any position can be affected. It is simply astounding the number of people in leadership positions (and those touting themselves as "leaders") who:

- Ignore or refuse to deal with complaints.
- Participate in harassment/bullying.
- Become annoyed when complaints are made.
- Fail to follow their own respectful workplace policies.
- Turn on the complainant and/or proceed to rid themselves of the complainant.
- Demean the stress and mental anguish of the person(s) affected.

I was and still am shocked and concerned about, among other things:

- Lack of understanding of what actions/factors constitute workplace bullying by everyone, particularly those within leadership positions. And, when this occurs:
  - How to address bullying effectively and properly.
  - Effects on the person being bullied, as well as on bystanders.
- Lack of concern and compassion for those being bullied by persons in leadership positions.
- Poorly conducted (or sham) investigations or no investigation at all.
- Targeting bullied employees for constructive dismissal.
- Use of non-disclosure agreements. Utilized frequently within some organizations to hide toxic culture. NDAs prevent the bullied from speaking out about their bullying experience(s) within the given organization(s).
- Destruction of careers of those targeted by bullies and/or toxic organizations.
  - Often followed by inability to secure future employment.

- The insidious nature of bullying (as stated by Linda Crockett of the Alberta Bullying Research Centre).
- Need for counselling for both those targeted and those who are bullying.

Deciding what to focus on first was the challenge. As you can imagine, there is a wealth of subject areas regarding bullying and harassment.

During the initial planning stages of the book, I recall speaking to my friend, Kari (you know who you are!). She discretely planted some seeds for thought, indicating that it would be impossible to include everything within one book. She told me to try to keep it focused and to think of a theme or target audience.

I wrestled with what to include over the next several months. Initially, I was set on providing numerous survivor stories. But, after stepping back, I decided to back up and provide information on the essentials of workplace bullying in this first book, starting at the beginning, and providing clarification on the insidious nature of bullying.

With this information, perhaps there might be a better understanding regarding the *insidiousness* of workplace bullying and harassment. With my experience (as well as those of numerous others I spoke with), there is a lack of understanding as to what workplace bullying and harassment really is. As the statistics later show, there is a general lack of follow-up and follow-through on any reported (whether verbally or any written form) cases of workplace bullying. Some people (and they even post on Facebook) disbelieve that workplace bullying exists. As a result, it is difficult for many to recognize it.

Linda Crockett is the founder of the Alberta Bullying Resource Centre.[1] I have spoken with and emailed Linda on my journey to understand my bullying experiences, as well as during the development of this book.

Perhaps this insidiousness is an underlying factor as to why workplace harassment and/or bullying is difficult to identify. It is deceiving and far more complex than most realize. It is prevalent throughout the world. Like a virus, it can permeate within businesses and grow.

---

1 For more information on the Alberta Bullying Resource Centre and Linda's mandate, please visit https://abrc.ca.

My inquisitive nature and concern over this misunderstood subject led me on a quest toward a better overall understanding of workplace bullying and harassment. Further to that, I wanted to provide others with better tools regarding workplace bullying and harassment.

There are numerous other people I spoke with via email regarding this phenomenon—people who had experienced workplace bullying first-hand, workplace investigators, lawyers, counsellors, and co-workers who had witnessed workplace harassment, to name a few.

To provide better insight and understanding of this widespread problem, I decided it was worthwhile beginning with defining and clarifying what workplace harassment and/or bullying actually is.

So, without further ado, let's get to it!

Section 1

Defining and Understanding Bullying and Harassment in the Workplace

CHAPTER 1:
Workplace Bullying & Harassment

Like the coronavirus, there are varying perceptions and beliefs regarding workplace bullying and/or harassment.

There are some people who are adamant that those speaking out about the subject are cry babies, too soft, thin-skinned, and so on. Should the topic be raised, employees speaking out about bullying or harassment are sometimes ridiculed, ostracized, and/or more or less told to suck it up. They are seen as the problem and told to grow up. There are sometimes suggestions to "Stand up for yourself." It is as simple as that. I, along with several others I have spoken to, have had acquaintances, previous co-workers, friends, and family who believe and state this. Some have actually been quite callous and rude about it.

I have finally come to terms with the non-believers' views. Their views are simply that: views. While I do not wish my experiences (or those of the abundance of others I have spoken with) on them, I still hold out hope that one day non-believers might understand there is more to workplace bullying and harassment than they currently see. However, when/if I have the reaction that I have previously had, I now realize and understand the phrase "these are not your people."

While it is fine for everyone to have their own views and opinions, we can all respect they will not necessarily be the same. That is part of what makes us all interesting. We can and should be able to discuss and understand varying viewpoints. But when/if someone is unreasonably rude, I have realized that I do not have to continue to associate with them or be around them, particularly when they are rude and/or demeaning. It isn't an easy thing to do, but sometimes it is necessary. I was actually quite shocked, hurt, and disappointed by the reactions of a few acquaintances and what they said. Part of getting healthier has helped me to better understand the choices we all have. Sometimes, we need to distance ourselves from others who are not supportive. And, frankly, this is the avenue I have had to take to preserve my mental health.

However, there are those in leadership positions who are also non-believers. Some people in leadership positions are irritated at the thought of what is sometimes referred to as babysitting or refereeing employees. Their suggestions may be for the employees to work it out between themselves. There is and can be frustration or irritation over the feeling that those in leadership positions have enough to tend to without having to deal with employees who are unable to work together.

On the plus side, there are authentic leaders who skilled at and knowledgeable about identifying workplace bullying and harassment. Not only do they identify it, but they also work proactively at ensuring a safe and respectful workplace for all employees. And, whether reported or not, they work diligently at eliminating workplace bullying and/or harassment.

People going through workplace bullying and/or harassment have a difficult enough time recognizing and believing what is going on. The shock, disbelief, and insidiousness of the methods employed by the bullies often leave the bullied discounting what they are experiencing. I still look back in disbelief at my whole experience.

This is why it is important to define workplace bullying and harassment.

There are a number of definitions of bullying and harassment. Most are similar to each other. While definitions are following, I would suggest checking legislation in your area for further clarification.

The following definition is from the Government of Canada website. Employees who fall under federal authority include those working in banks, airlines, railways, telecommunications, Aboriginal bands, interprovincial transportation, the post office, and radio and television stations.

Harassment

The Canadian (federal) definition of harassment is:

> improper conduct by an individual, that is directed at and offensive to another individual in the workplace, including at any event or any location related to work, and that the individual knew or ought reasonably to have known would cause offence or harm. It comprises objectionable act(s), comment(s) or display(s) that demean, belittle, or cause personal humiliation or embarrassment, and any act of intimidation or threat. It also includes harassment within the meaning of the *Canadian Human Rights Act* (i.e., based on race, national or ethnic origin, colour, religion, age, sex, sexual orientation, marital status, family status, disability and pardoned conviction).
>
> More specifically, harassment is normally a series of incidents but can be one severe incident which has a lasting impact on the individual. (Is it harassment? A tool to guide employees, 2015)

Some of these personal characteristics can include race, religion, ancestry, sex, sexual orientation, marital status, nationality, gender identity, mental or physical (dis)ability and age.

Following are just a few of the examples as to what may constitute harassment (as noted on the Government of Canada website):

- Preventing a person from expressing himself or herself: yelling at the person; threatening; constantly interrupting that person; prohibiting the person from speaking to others.

- Discrediting the person by spreading malicious gossip or rumours, ridiculing him/her, humiliating him/her, calling into question his/her convictions or his/her private life, shouting abuse at him/her.

- Isolating the person by no longer talking to him or her, denying or ignoring his or her presence, distancing him or her from others.

For a full the full list, please visit:

https://www.canada.ca/en/government/publicservice/wellness-inclusion-diversity-public-service/harassment-conflict-resolution/harassment-tool-employees.html

Following is a website from the Department of Labour in the United States regarding workplace harassment:

https://www.dol.gov/agencies/oasam/centers-offices/civil-rights-center/internal/policies/workplace-harassment/2012

As well, there are normally websites from each province in Canada, as well as each state in the United States.

For elsewhere in the world, I would suggest doing a web search with the key words of workplace, harassment and specifics of where you live and/or work.

Bullying

"Bullying is usually seen as acts or verbal comments that could psychologically or mentally hurt or isolate a person in the workplace. Sometimes, bullying can involve negative physical contact as well. Bullying usually involves repeated incidents or a pattern of behaviour that is intended to intimidate, offend, degrade, or humiliate a particular person or group of people. It has also been described as the assertion of power through aggression." (Canadian Centre for Occupational Health and Safety, 2021)

There is an immense number of tactics/examples utilized in bullying. Some people who have not experienced bullying are unable to comprehend the magnitude of the methods bullies employ.

> "While bullying is a form of aggression, the actions can be both obvious and subtle." (Canadian Centre for Occupational Health and Safety, 2021)

> "Bullying is usually considered to be a pattern of behaviour where one or more incidents will help show

that bullying is taking place." (Canadian Centre for Occupational Health and Safety, 2021)

The patterns of bullying behaviour may include a wide variety of tactics. Following are a few of these tactics, along with some examples.

Using Sexual Pressure

One of the first bullying strategies that comes to mind is *sexual pressure*. Thanks to the #METOO movement, there has been an awakening regarding this. Bill Cosby, Donald Trump, Harvey Weinstein, and Peter Nygard have recently been in the spotlight for sexual pressure, demands, comments, and innuendoes.

Intimidation

Intimidation is frequently used to suppress victims from speaking out. Acts of intimidation often include the job itself, promotions, or future opportunities.

Gossiping or Spreading Malicious Rumours

Sometimes there is gossip or malicious rumours. While there are differences between the two, many are unaware of the differences.

Gossiping is often referred to as office cooler talk. It is talking or discussing something or someone. It is considered as casual talk, without motive.

Rumours are a contrast to gossiping. They are spread with the intention to cause harm. A rumour seeks to spread unverified information.

A brief summary of the differences between gossip and rumours is:

> Gossip is a small talk with a person or with a group of people about something or someone without a specific purpose and goal. Rumor is a deliberate attempt to spread unproven facts or information about a person or thing with the intent to defame. (Difference between gossip and rumor, 2018)

Comments such as the following are bullying:

- "Is s/he the man or woman in the relationship?" (The bully focuses on the person's sexual orientation.)
- "S/he is a Bible thumper." (The bully refers to someone being religious. This can also be the opposite, where a religious person is persistently trying to convert a co-worker to a religion.)

General comments meant to discredit, undermine, alienate, or ridicule may include:

- "She's mentally unstable."
- "He's an idiot. He doesn't know what he's talking about."
- "She's too honest."

Being Condescending and Ridiculing

This type of bullying can be someone talking down toward someone or speaking to someone in a condescending tone and/or manner. This may be done in an attempt to make the bully appear superior.

Bullies may also make fun of various comments and/or ideas.

This type of bullying can be both subtle and outright obvious. A simple example I have seen was a supervisor and co-worker ridiculing another for referring to pants as slacks. Another example I've heard (an experienced) is calling a co-worker stupid.

Making Inappropriate Jokes

Most, if not all, of us have heard and seen a variety of inappropriate jokes. Sometimes these are targeted at a specific age, gender, race, or nationality.

Bullying can result in the *exclusion or isolation of someone*. Excluding someone can be subtle or obvious. Company get-togethers, such as picnics, office parties, or meetings are a few examples.

Exclusion from necessary training is yet another significant exclusion. This is discussed in detail in the case study in chapter 7.

Failure to Provide Resources or Information

Failing to provide training, procedures, policies, and updated information pertaining to the workplace are the most obvious.

Withholding information and resources is a more subtle form of this bullying strategy.

Unreasonable or Unfair Workloads

It is important that employers strive to be fair and consistent with workloads. While this is often a difficult measure to compare, there can be situations wherein it is quite noticeable.

An example in the chapter 7 case study illustrates this. Within the study, two co-workers alternate with the heavier workload. From the beginning, they were told to assist each other when the other had the heavier workload. Yet, while one assisted the other, this was not reciprocated. Often, it was refused in the presence of the supervisor, with no repercussions.

Undermining the Employee

This can include a wide range of actions. The bully may start false rumours, claim credit for a co-worker's work, scapegoat, gaslight, and/or sabotage their victim's work.

Sabotaging an Employee's Work

It may be difficult to perceive, but there are some employees who have gone and will go to such lengths as sabotaging another person's work.

This could be a project or a simple job that the co-worker has completed or is working on.

Changes are made to the project or work in progress to provide the appearance that the other person is incompetent.

Changing Work Guidelines

Every organization has guidelines. These are frequently used as general rules or principles to help/assist in guiding employees.

For example, an organization may have a general guideline for employees of a given department to assist others should they have a heavier workload.

If this guideline works for one, but not the other one(s), this is a changing guideline.

Setting Impossible Deadlines or Setting an Employee up for Failure

Deadlines are important. We all have them. But, when they are impossible or set up an employee to fail, there is a problem.

Clear and fair expectations for all should be a priority for everyone in leadership positions.

When an employee is given an impossible deadline to meet, it can be seen as setting an employee up for failure.

An example of this is provided in the case study in chapter 7.

Yelling and Using Profanity

During the course of writing this book, I have spoken to a variety of people in all types of positions. Employees of all positions and levels have had those in leadership positions yell at them and use profanity toward them.

Persistent Criticism

Constructive criticism can be helpful. We can learn and better ourselves when provided the opportunity. When criticism is presented constructively, it provides both the positives of what one is doing well, along with what areas can be improved upon.

Persistent criticism can fail to notice the good. If employees are singled out for persistent criticism that is intimidating and/or humiliating, it can be seen as bullying.

Micro-analyzing

When a bully micro-analyzes, they are analyzing various aspects of an employee's performance in an effort to find fault.

Providing constructive criticism to assist an employee to improve is fine. Doing so with the goal to discredit and/or constructively dismiss an employee is another. (See chapter 16 for more on this.) Chapter 7 provides another example of micro-analyzing.

Belittling an Employee's Opinions

As with any of the bullying examples, there are a variety of comments and methods used to belittle a target. Some comments include:

> "You are hopeless."

> "They are on their way out." (Referring to an employee.)

Constant Spying and Stalking

Tactics in this bullying strategy may include following/watching a co-worker to see where they go and what they are doing.

This can include watching to see how frequently they are going to the washroom and documenting how many breaks they take and the length of their breaks. Or this may include monitoring what programs (including work-related) and online activities the target uses and how often, or sometimes not. Bullies may undertake ongoing surveillance to verify their unsubstantiated claims against a co-worker.

It can include:

- Unwanted telephone calls, emails, or texts.
- Unwanted gifts.
- Following and/or watching a person. This can include co-workers, previous customer/client, former partner, or acquaintance. Regardless of who it is, they watch or follow the person's daily activities.
- Asking co-workers, friends, or family for contact information.
- Rifling through work desk and/or personal items.

Making False Accusations

False accusations may include anything from claiming a co-worker is working on coursework during company time, is shopping online, or is sexually harassing another employee.

Scapegoating

"Scapegoating is the practice of singling out a person or group for unmerited blame and consequent negative treatment." (Scapegoating, 2021)

A simple example is an employee blaming another employee for their mistakes.

Gaslighting

"Gaslighting is a form of psychological abuse where a person or group makes someone question their sanity, perception of reality, or memories. People experiencing gaslighting often feel confused, anxious, and unable to trust themselves." (Huizen, 2020)

One popular tactic often utilized by one gaslighting is DARVO, which is discussed in-depth in chapter 2.

CHAPTER 2:
DARVO

DARVO? When I first heard this term, I was puzzled. What the heck is DARVO?

The term DARVO was coined by psychologist Jennifer Freyd, PhD. She is a "psychology researcher, educator, and author. Her research on betrayal trauma and institutional courage have revolutionized the field of trauma psychology and the practice of institutional community-building" (Freyd, Biography, 2021).

Once I learned and understood it, DARVO was another revelation. It totally made sense. Much of what I was going through (covered in chapter 7) was classic DARVO. Prior to counselling and understanding DARVO, every single step in DARVO was utilized against me.

Although it often refers to sexual assaults, DARVO is also frequently used elsewhere, including the workplace. Some therapists see it as a form of gaslighting (DARVO, 2021). Or, as Jennifer Freyd states:

> I have observed that actual abusers threaten, bully and make a nightmare for anyone who holds them accountable or asks them to change their abusive behavior. This attack, intended to chill and terrify, typically includes threats of law suits, overt and covert attacks on the whistle-blower's credibility, and so on. The attack will often take the form of focusing on ridiculing the person who attempts to hold the offender accountable. [...] [T]he offender rapidly creates the impression

that the abuser is the wronged one, while the victim or concerned observer is the offender. Figure and ground are completely reversed. The more the offender is held accountable, the more wronged the offender claims to be. The offender is on the offense and the person attempting to hold the offender accountable is put on the defense. (1997)

The acronym DARVO describes a common strategy of abusers. DARVO stands for: Deny, Attack, and Reverse Victim and Offender.

The abuser will: **D**eny the abuse ever took place, then **A**ttack the victim for attempting to hold the abuser accountable; then they will lie and claim that they, the abuser, are the real victim in the situation, thus **R**eversing the **V**ictim and **O**ffender. (DARVO, 2021)

Interesting. Reading and discussing this concept was another eye-opener. And it made total sense once I researched and realized what it is.

Discussing this with others who had experienced workplace harassment and/or bullying, I discovered this whole DARVO phenomenon was more common than I had realized.

Examples of DARVO that are fairly easy to follow frequently involve situations often in the news, especially those regarding sexual harassment.

For a better understanding of this bullying tactic, I believe it is helpful to review each stage.

Deny

There is suspicion, concern, or awareness of something being off, being provided misinformation, being framed for mistakes not made, false rumours, and so on.

A multitude of scenarios (both others' and my own experiences) include statements such as:

- "I never said that."
- "I didn't tell you that."

- "You are crazy."
- "It was just a joke."
- "You are blowing it out of proportion."
- "It wasn't that big of a deal."

Doing so often throws off both the person being attacked/bullied, as well as anyone in an authority or leadership position to whom this is being reported.

The deny stage then opens up the ability for the bully or attacker to further add to this by then attacking the complainant/target to discredit them.

Attack

Attacking the complainant/target with the intention to discredit the person/employee complaining can be done in a number of ways, including claiming that the co-worker:

- is a whiner, a liar, or stupid.
- has mental health issues.
- is not a good fit.
- has performance issues.
- is not accountable.[2]

Other tactics include gossiping about the employee, making up false stories about the employee or about what the employee has said, and/or providing the employee with false procedures or information.

"Mine" mentality can also be involved. Here, the bully tells the targeted employee that the bully is next in line for any promotions. They have been there longer, and just because the bullied employee is more

---

[2] This often occurs when the bully is the guilty party, the one who isn't actually being accountable.

educated and/or taking courses on their own doesn't mean the bullied employee can "come in here and take what's mine," according to the bully.

Finally, the bullied person may be blamed for being alienated, excluded, and/or exiled for telling on them. The bully may say things like:

- "I was mad at you for telling them what I did."
- "I was upset at you because you _____."
- "I wouldn't have treated you that way if you didn't tell on me."
- "You provoked me."

In other words, "Because you did this, I did that." See the case study in chapter 7 for a detailed example.

Reverse Victim and Offender

In this stage, the offender will attempt to ensure the targeted employee appears to be incompetent, mentally unstable, have performance issues, and/or any other problems.

Essentially, the bully blames the target for mistakes made by themselves. This may occur with little to no proof, and when the victim asks for clarification, they may be further attacked.

The bully will tell other co-workers or departments that the target made the error(s), when this was not the case. This can occur despite evidence to the contrary, or even other co-workers witnessing the bully make the mistake(s) themselves.

The bully may take on a spying/stalking role, providing their supervisor with frequent "updates" regarding the person they are, in fact, targeting. These might take various forms, including details about the target's actions while at work and documentation of even the tiniest of errors.

CHAPTER 3:

Human Rights in Canada

I would be remiss if I did not include examples of what may be considered human rights violations.

As noted on the Canadian Human Rights Commission's website, the rights protected by the Canadian Human Rights Act "stem from the Universal Declaration of Human Rights" (Human rights in Canada, 2020).

The Universal Declaration of Human Rights includes a list of 30 articles. These articles are what shape human rights. This declaration includes articles on equality and freedom from discrimination.

The Canadian Human Rights Act covers all individuals under federal jurisdiction. This includes those employed by the federal government, regulated by the federal government, or receiving services from the federal government. Some of these include First Nations governments, banks, broadcasters, and telecommunications companies.

> Provincial or territorial human rights laws are very similar to the Canadian Human Rights Act and apply many of the same principles. They protect people from discrimination in areas of provincial and territorial jurisdiction, such as restaurants, stores, schools, housing and most workplaces. (Human rights in Canada, 2020)

If you do not fall under federal jurisdiction in Canada, and live elsewhere than Manitoba, a web search can quickly provide you the human rights information for your province. Current links for each province are provided in the appendix.

If you live elsewhere in the world, I encourage you to do the same. Including terms such as "human rights" and where you live is a good place to start.

For those living in Manitoba, Canada, following is brief information on human rights in Canada, along with the website of where to look.

Human Rights in Manitoba are governed by the Manitoba Human Rights Commission.

Their website defines discrimination as follows:

Discrimination is treating a person differently, to their disadvantage where it is not reasonable to do so on the basis of their:

- ancestry, including colour and perceived race
- nationality or national origin
- ethnic background or origin
- religion, religious belief, association or activity
- age
- sex, including pregnancy
- gender identity
- sexual orientation
- marital or family status
- source of income
- political belief, association or activity
- physical or mental disability
- social disadvantage (Province of Manitoba | v1, 2020)

Under the Canadian Human Rights Act, there are 13 grounds for discrimination:

- Race
- National or Ethnic Origin
- Colour

- Religion
- Age
- Sex
- Sexual Orientation
- Gender Identity or Expression
- Marital Status
- Family Status
- Disability
- Genetic Characteristics
- A conviction for which a pardon has been granted or a record suspended (What is discrimination?, 2020)

CHAPTER 4:
Schoolyard vs. Workplace Bullies

Most of us are aware of various tactics bullies (both schoolyard and workplace) can and do employ. Regardless of whether they are schoolyard or workplace bullies, common characteristics of bullies include:

- Insecurity
- Low self-esteem
- Lack of empathy
- Manipulative behaviour
- Condescension

"Bullies harass others based on their own issues related to self-esteem and inadequacy" (Badzmierowski, 2016).

To further understand workplace bullying or harassment, it is important to know that while there are similarities, there are also noticeable difference between schoolyard and workplace bullies.

A schoolyard bully perceives their target as weaker, different, or not fitting in. Some examples of these perceptions include learning challenges, social status, and physical size.

Case Study: What Do You Do When Your Child is Bullied?

Learning challenges can encompass a wide range. As a parent of a special needs child, I can relate to this. The child bullying my daughter also had learning challenges and insecurity issues. However, their challenges or disabilities were not as pronounced as those of my daughter.

Despite overcoming enormous challenges, my daughter is noticeably challenged. Besides being unable to walk until she was about seven years old, she is primarily non-verbal and mentally behind. Both she and her bully rode the school bus daily. And, daily, he would torment her.

As with many children, the bully would move around on the bus. My daughter, due to her low muscle tone, was in a seat belt. This meant he would go to her and taunt her.

This culminated with her seeing what appeared to be an exchange of money and pills between two other children on the bus. After a few hours of interrogation and specific details, I suggested that she speak to a teacher and/or teacher's aid.

The following day, she did as I indicated. With the help of her teacher's aid, she indicated what she saw, along with further details on the ongoing bullying.

Instead of commending her for coming forward and doing the right thing, my daughter was condemned and made to apologize to the bully for accusing him. She came home that day upset. And, as often is the case, it took me several hours to settle her down.

I felt terrible. Here, as a parent, I had encouraged my daughter to do what I thought was right. But the response she received was not one that would encourage anyone to come forward with any concerns.

The following school day, my husband and I advised the principal and vice principal we were coming in to speak with them. For me to confront any teacher, let alone a principal, was a huge thing. I grew up as a principal's daughter, and tried to respect the tough position teachers and principals were in. However, what had happened to our daughter was unacceptable.

When we met with them, there were a number of excuses. They felt sorry for the other child. There were already a lot of complaints against him. When they said they didn't want to "set him back," I looked at them in shock and asked, "Is it okay for our daughter to be set back?" For her, little things often did set her back.

The other commented, "Neither of the kids are angels."

We calmly but firmly told them, "We have always attempted to work WITH the school and her assistants, teachers, and anyone that she/we dealt with. And, when she misbehaves, we try to act on it." One of those times was when she got upset with the bully and retaliated by throwing something at him. We took her to his place and made her sign/apologize for her actions.

We were in shock. But, prior to leaving, they did acknowledge problems/concerns with drugs, and they were going to have a dog come in at a later date to sniff things out.

From there, we left and discovered the bullying had been going on longer than we were aware.

After my husband spoke to another young girl on the bus, we discovered just how severe it was. We were, and still are, extremely grateful and impressed with the young lady's honesty and courage to tell my husband what had been happening.

We found out that it had been going on for a few months. The bully was kicking her feet, poking her, and saying unspeakably terrible things, including suggestions that she end her life.

When we spoke to a few of her cousins, who were also on the bus, we discovered they were also aware.

At one point, one of them told the bully to leave her alone. After that, she began to get threatening texts from the bully's sister, who we were advised was living with someone on house arrest. When asked why they didn't say anything, we were told that their parents had advised them to stay out of it.

I was in complete shock. How could anyone throw anyone else under the bus like that? Let alone someone who is your cousin and has extra needs. We were upset and hurt. And we felt sick over how our daughter had to endure this. Looking back upon this after my experiences, I can't help but further understand the terminology of "Bystander Effect". For further understanding on this, there is an article included in the appendix regarding this.

When my husband tried to speak to the bully's father, the man blew up and said, "Why is everyone picking on my kid?"

Another shock, and a poor way to deal with behaviour issues. Leaving anyone, child or adult, unaccountable for unacceptable behaviour allows that behaviour to become permissible and will continue into adulthood. Left to continue, these people often can and do bully within the workplace.

Workplace Bullies

Upon entering the workforce, a workplace bully is often threatened by the person they are targeting. This may be due to the other person's skills and knowledge, capabilities, integrity, morals, and/or non-confrontational behaviour. In short, employees displaying competence with a conscience may be recipients of bullying. As a result, the workplace bully may see their target as competition that needs to be stifled, destroyed, or removed.

There are countless, unimaginable workplace harassment stories, stories I had originally wanted to include.

There are also just as many reasons I did not include some of the numerous and unacceptable workplace bullying stories. Some of the victims are not prepared to speak about their experiences. Others have signed non-disclosure agreements. A few are afraid to speak up for fear of further retaliation. And, often, there are some (as with myself and many I know) who experience tremendous difficulties obtaining future employment after attempting to speak out. The bullying often continues, even after the victim has left the toxic workplace.

Next, we look at how the tactics of both schoolyard bullies and workplace bullies can be and are similar. Both schoolyard and workplace bullies tend to have self-esteem and inadequacy issues. These insecurities can lead either kind of bully to employ similar tactics. The following chapter is Dr. Gary Namie's article on the top 25 tactics employed by bullies, which I found spot-on.

CHAPTER 5:
"Top 25 Tactics Adopted by all Bullies"

By Dr. Gary Namie, Workplace Bullying Institute (www.workplacebullying.org)

- Falsely accused someone of "errors" not actually made (71%)
- Stared, glared, was nonverbally intimidating and was clearly showing hostility (68%)
- Discounted the person's thoughts or feelings ("oh, that's silly") in meetings (64%)
- Used the "silent treatment" to "ice out" & separate from others (64%)
- Exhibited presumably uncontrollable mood swings in front of the group (61%)
- Made up own rules on the fly that even she/he did not follow (61%)
- Disregarded satisfactory or exemplary quality of completed work despite evidence (58%)
- Harshly and constantly criticized having a different "standard" for the Target (57%)
- Started, or failed to stop, destructive rumors or gossip about the person (56%)

- Encouraged people to turn against the person being tormented (55%)
- Singled out and isolated one person from coworkers, either socially or physically (54%)
- Publicly displayed "gross," undignified, but not illegal, behavior (53%)
- Yelled, screamed, threw tantrums in front of others to humiliate a person (53%)
- Stole credit for work done by others (47%)
- Abused the evaluation process by lying about the person's performance (46%)
- "Insubordinate" for failing to follow arbitrary commands (46%)
- Used confidential information about a person to humiliate privately or publicly (45%)
- Retaliated against the person after a complaint was filed (45%)
- Made verbal put-downs/insults based on gender, race, accent or language, disability (44%)
- Assigned undesirable work as punishment (44%)
- Made undoable demands (workload, deadlines, duties) for person singled out (44%)
- Launched a baseless campaign to oust the person and not stopped by the employer (43%)
- Encouraged the person to quit or transfer rather than to face more mistreatment (43%)
- Sabotaged the person's contribution to a team goal and reward (41%)
- Ensured failure of person's project by not performing required tasks: signoffs, taking calls, working with collaborators (40%)

Regardless of the position of the perpetrator/bully, the tactics employed are frequently done discretely. Bullies are often seen as gifted or master manipulators. Therefore, recognizing disrespectful behaviour can be difficult to identify.

It is vital for anyone in leadership positions to understand and recognize signs of bullies, as well as those being targeted.

As I work on another edit on this book, Dr. Namie released details on an updated workplace bullying survey. Some of this updated information is included below.

What Stopped the Bullying

67% Targeted employees have a 67% chance of losing the jobs they loved for no legitimate reason.

23% Target voluntarily left the job to escape more mistreatment.

17% Target was forced to quit when work conditions were deliberately made intolerable.

15% Target transferred to different job or location with same employer.

12% Employer terminated the target.

12% It did not stop.

11% Perpetrator was punished but kept job.

9% Perpetrator was terminated.

6% Positive actions by employer stopped it.

4% Positive actions by target's co-workers stopped it.

3% Perpetrator voluntarily quit.

Further details on this comprehensive report completed by the Workplace Bullying Institute can be found at https://workplacebullying.org/2021-wbi-survey/

There are numerous other statistics within this valuable survey, as well as on the website above.

CHAPTER 6:

Signs of Bullying in the Workplace

As with many, I was unaware there could be indicators of bullying in the workplace. Perhaps I falsely believed it was just a schoolyard issue. In fact, I looked forward to growing up.

But I assumed incorrectly. I discovered that bullying wasn't just a schoolyard occurrence. No one should have to deal with bullying in any shape or form.

I am pleased to see that there appears to be more knowledge, recognition, and attempts to deal with schoolyard bullying. There is more media attention, better education, and increased counselling availability. Yet, there is room for improvement, as there is with regard to workplace bullying.

Media coverage of workplace bullying is increasing. But it has significant strides to make. While we keep hearing about zero tolerance and respectful workplace policies, the bullying continues.

Regardless of where anyone lives in the world, we can all do better. Bullying is simply unacceptable.

To start with, it is helpful for anyone to better understand what indicators may be useful to watch for. These indicators can better help to alert anyone if and when a bully may be within your workplace.

Regardless of your position in the workplace, I urge you to be willing to stand up to any kind of bullying. If you are a co-worker, be willing and prepared to speak out against poor behaviour. As an employer (whatever capacity it may be—owner, partner, supervisor, manager, etc.), show your leadership abilities and ensure you have a safe and healthy workplace. Follow up and through on *all* disrespectful behaviour, whether reported or not. Be willing to call the bullying what it is. Things may not always be what they appear.

There are a number of indicators that a person in a leadership position can watch for. As noted previously, these are often trivialized by some and can become everyday occurrences within toxic environments, normalizing this kind of behaviour. Yet, this is not normal behaviour.

- Frequent updates on employee's performance.[3]
- Unreasonable demands upon co-worker/employee.
- Undermining comments regarding employee.
- Blaming others for mistakes.
- Refusing to assist another co-worker, yet demanding assistance from said co-worker when needed.
- Encouraging the omission of targeted employee from meetings, training, etc. on the premise they haven't completed work, are "too slow," etc.
- Taking credit for others' successes.
- Eye rolling/ gestures/ rude comments toward targeted employee.
- Interrupting target.
- Belittling target.
- Gossiping about target.

---

[3] This can be confusing, as there are also those that genuinely are providing needed feedback on a problematic employee. A skilled, non-biased leader should be adept at knowing the difference. And there are normally other key factors besides the frequent updates on performance.

Workplace Bullying

With the existing pandemic and many continuing to work remotely from home at least part-time, some might think this would at least pause bullying or harassment. But this is sadly not the case.

Workplace bullying or harassment has adapted. Some of the signs are the same or similar. Others are different and/or a little more covert. Those in leadership positions and bystanders also need to be acutely aware of various signs even during the pandemic.

Indications of bullying while working remotely may include:

- Eye rolling, snickering, or rude gestures during a meeting (Zoom, Skype, etc.).
- Texting each other (on one another's cells, for example) while on virtual (Zoom, Skype) meetings.[4]
- Deliberately excluding or "missing" someone from group emails.
- Additional expectations or demands from co-workers and/or employer. This may include texting, calling, or emailing before and/or after hours with the expectation of replies.
- Screenshot(s) shared during meeting with disparaging comments, remarks, or confidential information on an employee. (This is often another form of undermining another person's abilities.)
- Interrupting someone while they are speaking.
- Making disparaging comments regarding another co-worker, supervisor, or employee on any social media.
- Sending offensive emails or threats.

Regardless of the type or form of bullying, it is vitally important for all involved that it be addressed. Reports, whether verbal or written, need to be addressed. Sometimes, employees may not realize their actions are considered bullying. Others do. Both need to be aware of the consequences of their behaviour, along with the follow-up and follow-through

---

4 It is not always easily noticeable. Yet, at times, some employees will text back and forth making rude comments/remarks regarding other employees in the meeting and/or the person hosting the meeting, for example. Or they may make inappropriate comments (or texts, emails) aimed at another's appearance (body, clothing, etc.)

procedures. Persons bullying who are willing to address their behaviour and change can also be supported with counselling and follow-up with leadership, including their supervisor(s) and HR.

Persons targeted need to be supported by supervisors and HR. The person(s) targeted need support from supervisor(s), HR, (hopefully) bystanders, and co-workers, and have counselling programs made available to them.

Recognizing the indications of bullying aids leadership in addressing workplace harassment and bullying that may currently be overlooked. For bullying behaviours that are overlooked, there are various signs that can often indicate an employee is being bullied and/or harassed. These indications are often coping mechanisms of a person being targeted.

Signs and indications of a harassed or bullied employee(s) may include:

- Isolation (by themselves and/or others).
- Becoming withdrawn.
- Confusion and/or frustration.
- Anxiety and panic attacks.
- Being overly emotional.
- Change in behaviour and/or performance.
- Silence when the employee would previously raise concerns. The employee no longer participates and/or raises issues.
- Appears to have given up.
- Increased, or appearance of increased, errors.
- Increased absenteeism.

Also, if or when the employee attempts to write a formal request for an investigation into workplace bullying and/or request something be done about workplace bullying, it may appear overly emotional and lengthy, as was the case with mine.

Overly emotional letters are often a desperate plea for help and for someone to hear concerns that have failed to be addressed.

In addition, a key indicator of workplace bullying is noticeably high staff turnover, whether within a given department or in an organization as a whole.

Organizations suffering from poor leadership tend to find issue with the targeted employee. It is easier to label an employee as a problem employee, a complainer, a mental case, a poor choice, not a fit, disgruntled, and so on. Poor leadership will usually choose not to deal with workplace bullying and/or harassment. Instead, they will often avoid dealing with the bullying and/or harassment within. They will often rid themselves of the complaining employee. Avoiding the root causes of bullying and/or harassment further entrenches the unhealthy bullying and harassment behaviours within.

An authentic leader fosters and encourages healthy organizations. They watch for, recognize, question, and concern themselves with the possibility of any harassed and/or bullied employee. Coworkers are encouraged to speak out, whether in the particular department or not.

For further clarification, following are examples from my personal experience of common tactics employed in a toxic workplace.

Exclusion from necessary training is a significant exclusion. This is one that stands out for me.

Following are examples of workplace and organizational behaviour that may cause employees some discomfort, but which are *not* bullying or harassment.

- Expressions of differences of opinion.
- Following up on absences from work.
- Fair allocation of work.
- Bantering, joking around (but these can quickly cross the line) by employer or co-worker(s).
- Bad day by boss or co-worker(s), sometimes referred to as "one offs."
- *Fair* and *objective* feedback.
    - *This is feedback that is free of someone else's opinions and suggestions. As a person within a leadership position, it is*

important to form your own independent judgments. If you are providing any feedback, it is important to at least try to be consistent with all employees.

- *Reasonable* action by an employer and/or supervisor to assess, evaluate, transfer, demote, discipline, or dismiss an employee. This *may* include:
  - *properly* and *fairly* performed performance management (i.e., progressive discipline; see chapter 14).
  - honest and fair appraisals.

Understanding bullying and harassment is important for everyone. All too often, it continues to be trivialized, but for those attempting to address it, it is no laughing matter.

For anyone looking for further assistance and information, there is additional material in the appendix.

CHAPTER 7:
Case Study – One of my Experiences Being Bullied

All Names have been changed
Tonya (Deputy Director – later Director of Human Resources)
Lorena (Supervisor)
Jane (Co-Worker)
Elvira (Current Director of Human Resources)
Stan (Safety Officer)

Initially, I felt privileged and excited about obtaining a payroll administrator opportunity within a city of approximately 50,000 people. I have always enjoyed a challenge and was proud of my excellent work habits, with past performance evaluations showing this.

As I was eager to start fresh, I dove at the opportunity. I had already walked away from a toxic workplace, one that had already garnered significant staff departures and media attention.

When I started telling people of my new opportunity, there were a few who had negative remarks and said, "It is not a nice/good place to work." I dismissed their comments, thinking that if I went in with a positive attitude and my good work ethic, I would be fine.

Besides signing the usual offer of employment, my supervisor, Lorena and I went over a progression plan. This plan noted the agreement between myself and the city to continue the required courses for the designation of payroll compliance practitioner (PCP). A university course I was taking was one of the required courses. Following that, I took the next one required, with the city reimbursing me for the cost.

The disparaging comments from the onset by Jane (my co-worker), about Lorena (the supervisor), co-workers, and directors surprised me. Regardless of who they were, they were subject to both her and her husband's criticism. Comments on their lack of abilities, education, knowledge, and experience were frequent, as were comments about how Jane (or her husband) should have someone's position, how she should have a raise, or how her husband would do a better job than others in positions, regardless of whether he (or she) had the necessary education or experience.

Lorena, Elvira (the current director of human resources), and (Tonya) (currently deputy director) were frequently ridiculed by Jane. She speculated about abilities or lack thereof, how people attained their positions, or how they were dressed. Her disdain for Lorena having previously written her up and/or given her an ROD (Record of Discussion) was another sore point. Jane frequently commented on Lorena's inability to handle stress, her moodiness, constant talk of her children, complaining, and blocking of ability to take vacation in a time she wanted to take vacation.

I recall a particular conversation with this previous co-worker regarding the current deputy director (later director) of human resources. Comments were made regarding what she claimed to be recent and and previous waitress experience and where. As well, there were comments on her time as a 911 operator, connections to the later city manager, and her relationship (even later) with the fire chief. Speculations on how/why she was promoted to a director position within the fire department were made. And, there were comments regarding her time as a 911 operator, connections to the later city manager, and then the fire chief. Speculations on how/why she was promoted to a director position within the fire department were made. And, how this same co-worker felt her husband could do a better job as the director. Further speculation was made on why/how she was then transferred to the deputy director position and was being groomed to move to director of human resources. Coincidentally , she (the deputy director) was taking her coursework online through the same university as I was.

While speaking directly to each of these people, Jane's disposition was much more congenial. There was flattery toward almost anything, including clothing, appearance, family, and work. As Stan (a safety officer) stated, Jane knew how to pour on the sugar and she knew they liked it. Stan also commented on how Lorena "lapped it up."

I would later replay a comment in my head made by Stan, regarding workplace health and safety and workers' compensation benefits (WCB). He openly admitted how easy it was to convince this WCB and Workplace Safety and Health that any employee affected was responsible in some way. Often it was due to "failure to follow a procedure or policy." Or, in his own words, sometimes he would "throw them a bone." And they might receive a small fine.

This revelation shocked and saddened me. I could not understand how this was acceptable. I watched in marvel at Jane's smoothness and how it did not appear obvious to some of the others. So, I was surprised when Stan noticed, and commented on how she would butter up Lorena or anyone (including Tonya) when she wanted something.

There were a few luncheon meetings that I was initially excited and proud to be allowed to attend. I was intrigued by the number of politicians, business owners, and people in higher positions who attended these functions.

Jane spoke about some of the people in attendance, the ice cream place her husband owned and ran, and how they knew some of the people (including the city manager). She also spoke of how the current city manager and his family would come in for ice cream. Jane also commented on her surprise when he and his wife separated. It was later noted by other former staff how Tonya and her fire chief boyfriend assisted the city manager when he moved.

Both Elvira and Tonya would freely note how they would write a variety of letters on behalf of the city manager.

There were various discussions between Lorena & Jane. A few previous employees were discussed, in addition to the one who had requested to be transferred prior to me. They were ridiculed for being incompetent, having "issues," or constantly making errors.

There was no formal training. The processes within payroll were similar every other week. One week was the input and update of information. This was primarily entering new information normally received from a staff change notice (SCN). Some of this information included new employees, moves to other departments, layoffs, pay increases, and benefits. The alternate week was verifying payroll and processing pay. I recall being handed a pile of employee payroll and pay reports for that pay period and advised to go through them. I asked for more specifics to understand more thoroughly what I needed to watch for. I received a vague answer regarding checking hours for each area, benefits, and pay rate.

There were several hundred employees, along with various departments. Many, but not all, employees were covered by a union. There were several unions and contracts to become familiar with. There were benefits and rates to understand. There were processes involved with their staff change notices, how the filing system worked, electronic filing, and so on.

I jumped in and worked at reviewing and understanding every aspect of the job I could. I reviewed the various contracts to become more familiar with each of them. I went through anything I could find to understand the workings of the organization, each department, diverse hours of work for the numerous departments involved, pay scales, and so on. While I normally attempted to find the answers or dig for information prior to asking questions, I would follow up with questions if I was unsure. Any questions would often result in eyerolling, sighs, admonitions to read the GOG (general operating guide), some other gesture, and sometimes a remark to figure it out on my own.

The GOG was not formal. These were guidelines on a variety of things that were randomly produced by anyone (Tonya or Jane, etc.). An example included the steps for running payroll for the existing and the upcoming new payroll system.

With the lack of specifics, I began a manual of my own to which I could refer. I not only took some of these GOGs to expand on, but also wrote my own notes on guidelines and practices to follow. I had this on my computer desktop. It basically covered everything and anything one would need to know regarding the position. I had done this in previous positions and places of employment. One of them, I was told over 10 years later, was still being utilized to assist in training staff.

During my first week, my experience and education was commented on by Jane. Apparently, she had the understanding that I had little experience or ongoing/further education in payroll. I informed her of ongoing and previous courses I had taken and was currently taking. As well, I had experience with other aspects of payroll and human resources (scheduling, administrative, benefits). I explained that I would be finishing my payroll courses and was continuing to finish my human resources certificate online. Jane responded by informing me that she had been there around five years and was next in line for either human resources or the payroll supervisor position. She had no plans on doing further education, particularly if it was on her own time and/or cost.

After that discussion, Jane constantly accused me of working on my course during work hours. I would leave a separate browser window ready and waiting for my coffee break times and lunch to work on. When I needed the internet for work purposes, this browser with the university log-in, would pop up. Immediately, Jane would yell out and claim I was working on my course. As we sat fairly close, she could see my computer screen. Each time she would accuse me, I would try to tell Jane and Lorena that it was simply my browser I had ready for my coffees and/or lunch time. Regardless, Jane continued to accuse me and even went to Tonya with her complaint.

The second required course I enrolled in while working with the city I did as I had done previously. I enrolled and paid the applicable fees. I provided the copy of the fees to Lorena. She did not respond immediately, so I asked again. However, this time, Lorena claimed I had not verified with her prior and they would not reimburse me. I was stunned. At no time was I told that it had to be pre-authorized. It was in the progression plan, of which I tried to remind her. She then said she would double-check with Tonya. Both Lorena & Tonya continued to refuse to reimburse me for this regardless.

Jane and Lorena would spend a significant amount of time shopping online and on Facebook. They would talk about the various Facebook buy and sell sites, other shopping websites, and order items together or separately. There were games on their phones they enjoyed playing. One of the favourites was Pokémon, which was also played while at work. One of them was excited when they found a Pokémon within the building during work time.

The week of input and update was divided into two groupings. One was a heavier workload than the other, and I was advised by Lorena and Jane that whoever had the lighter load was to assist the other with the heavier workload once they completed theirs. There were several times when I was not only presented with more, but also offered assistance. Yet, when I had the heavier workload, I was not provided the same courtesy. I was often advised to do it myself by Jane, both in the presence of Lorena and not. There were many times where I worked through coffee breaks, came in early, worked through some of my lunch, and/or stayed later to complete what needed to be done.

After the week of entering and updating information was completed, we were to go over each other's completed work to ensure accuracy. All of the folders of each area we completed were swapped over to be reviewed. As well, the reports of pending payroll were verified.

After payroll was run and complete, we then had the task of scanning and electronically filing all of the work completed. While Jane had a large stack of unscanned paperwork that had accumulated, I preferred to have this completed in a timely manner. A few days after one of the runs, the folders of work I had completed were still scattered across Jane's desk. I had to request a few times before finally receiving them. Once I received them, I promptly began scanning them in order to electronically file them.

Unfortunately, I failed to notice that some contracts for employees had been returned reversed. As a result, I scanned and electronically filed them into the wrong employee file. That error, along with other errors, were typed out and presented to me on a record of discussion

(ROD) in May 2016. There was no prior discussion on presumed errors. These presumed errors were procedures that I had been advised on by Jane, which were apparently inaccurate. I asked if I could have my say. Lorena looked shocked at the idea and said OK. I wrote my responses. Lorena photocopied and gave me a copy. I fixed the misfiling and apologized and admitted that perhaps my recent events (my mother's death and our house fire) had played a role. The misfiling was the week after the fire. I took responsibility and apologized for letting my personal life affect my performance. When I met with Tonya regarding this and being upset over the ROD, it was commented that I was making excuses.

The house fire occurred on a Friday. I was busy taking care of estate business for my mother, when I received the Bluetooth call from my husband. We had planned a snowmobile get away with another couple and had our special needs daughter set up with respite for the weekend. I could tell by my husband's voice that something was wrong, so I asked. His response was that I should come home as the house was on fire.

I went directly back to the office and informed Jane of the situation and that I was going home. That same afternoon, the payroll and human resource department were celebrating another co-worker's birthday and were all enjoying some ice cream cake and visiting. I had a few texts from Lorena asking about the fire and sent a few pictures.

Upon return to work on Monday, the most pressing concern from both Lorena & Jane was whether I planned on taking vacation or banked time for the afternoon I was off due to the fire.

Shortly after this, Jane went on a two-week vacation. During this time, both Lorena and I had found and corrected numerous errors by Jane. Additionally, a human resource assistant came into the office and advised the Lorena about a few employees who had had their information electronically filed into each other's files by Jane. Upon my Jane's return, she was simply verbally advised about the misfiling by Lorena and told to correct it.

After payroll was sent, the following payroll timeframes, along with their respective groups, needed to be set up in advance. There were times when I would do this, but Jane claimed to have done so. This would normally be done in front of Lorena. When I tried to correct her on this (as well as other situations), most of the time, she would deny it.

On one particular occasion, Lorena and Jane had taken coffee together and left for lunch while I was sending payroll. After I finished sending payroll, I had the opportunity to have lunch out with my husband, who had just happened to come to town. I sent a text to the supervisor to indicate I would appreciate taking my coffee and lunch together due to this. I received a condescending text back advising I needed to ask to do so in advance. As a result, I took take-out instead and returned. Upon my return, both Lorena and Jane glared at me and barely spoke to me the rest of the day.

The alternate week when payroll was being processed, the pay needed to be processed and sent to the bank in a timely manner. If it was late being sent, employees might not receive their pay on time. On a few occasions, I was left with the task of sending some of the payroll very close to the timeline. Sometimes, I ended up working through my morning coffee and into lunch, if and when I was left to run the last payroll with a very limited timeframe. Another time (during processing), Jane unexpectedly took time off to take some practice photography pictures for a grade 12 class graduation of which her son was in. This again meant working through coffee and lunch in order to meet the timeframe required. None of this time was acknowledged or compensated.

Time off for funerals was to be at the supervisor's discretion. I made arrangements with Lorena to attend a funeral. As I live out of town, and both my husband and I planned to attend, he drove me to work (45 miles away) and picked me up at noon. The funeral was at 1 p.m. and we planned to have lunch and then attend the funeral. Jane was off on vacation, so I made a deal with Lorena to stay late the night prior to ensure the work was completed. During this time, Jane came in and asked why I was there. I informed her of the funeral and my appreciation towards Lorena for the ability to make arrangements to go. Jane's animosity towards me was clear that evening. She was inquisitive regarding the time of the funeral, how long I was taking off, and if I was returning afterwards. Jane noted she had emails she needed to send, and once finished, she left abruptly.

The following day, I commented that Jane had been in, and Lorena had noted receiving email(s). Lorena then went on to question me if I would be returning to work following the funeral, despite our previous arrangements and being aware my husband had driven me to work. I told her I was not sure how long the funeral would be. Then I mentioned I had stayed a few hours late the previous night, and had made prior arrangements with her to take the afternoon off.

My husband was shocked and upset over the sudden change in arrangements, as was I. I stressed the whole time about returning afterwards. But, as it was a rather large funeral, and many were still coming in at the start time, it was late beginning. The funeral was for a friend's mother. We wanted to give our condolences. By the time it was over, it was pretty much the end of the work day. Needless to say, I did not return to work.

The following day, both Lorena and Jane questioned me as to why I did not return. I tried to explain. They barely spoke to me that day.

My work guidelines were frequently changed. As Jane was more senior, I was expected to rely on her or Lorena for information. Often, I would be told to perform duties, only to be questioned by Jane or Lorena as to why I had done it that way. Upon claiming it was what I was told, Jane or Lorena would gaslight me by:

- Claiming I was wrong, dreaming, making it up.
- Deny I was told that procedure.
- Tell me I was not being accountable.

While Jane and Lorena were gone to a payroll conference, the person previously in my position came to assist with my training and with payroll. During this time, she acknowledged the toxic atmosphere and that she had requested a transfer out. She told me to email her anytime if I had questions about procedures. There was acknowledgement of both Jane and Lorena as being problematic, but she had had more of a problem with Lorena. Yet, she did admit Jane was difficult to work with. In addition, some of the information I was provided was not entirely correct. What I had not realized was that this person and Jane had what some would refer to as a love–hate friendship.

Not long after Jane and Lorena returned from the conference, I was unsure of a procedure advised by Jane. When I tried to ask for further clarification, I was glared at and just told to do it that way. Wanting a better understanding, I emailed the previous payroll employee to provide me the answer and determine if I had been advised properly. Within a day, Jane came back to the office after visiting with this person. Jane had found out that I had questioned her. Jane was very vocal to me, Lorena, and everyone around. I was verbally reprimanded by both Jane and Lorena for doing so.

Besides this, I had suspected Jane of lying about her mistakes, and framing me for her mistakes. It appeared that every mistake that occurred was mine. Anytime I raised a question, I was told I was not being accountable. If I ever dared to advise her of an error, I was told to fix it.

Also, during this time, a new payroll program was being implemented. While this was being set up, this meant double entering everything regarding payroll. There was a lot of work involved to ensure the transition from one payroll program to another went as smoothly as possible. Ensuring every employee was set up correctly and following each respective contract (including pay rates, benefits, and much more) were part of this. Lorena was working directly with the new payroll program company and their representatives.

Prior to Lorena's vacations, I had heard that a good friend of Tonya's was going to be doing a few training sessions on the new payroll program being implemented. She had been working together with Lorena, Tonya, and those with the new payroll program company to set this up. I was looking forward to learning about the program.

During this week, I had the heavier workload. Additionally, there were larger than normal layoffs due to the time of year. As usual, Jane refused to assist with the workload. What I had not realized was that Jane convinced Lorena to omit me from the training being provided to numerous clerks, payroll input personnel, and themselves. Had I not noticed them preparing for the training and about to leave, I would have missed the training. I asked Lorena why I was being excluded. The answer came from Jane (and in front of Lorena), telling me I had too much work that needed to be completed. Upon questioning how I was expected to know or understand the new system without attending the training, I was allowed to participate. Jane made the obvious point of sitting as far away from me as possible in the training room. I then worked through some coffees and lunches to ensure my workload was completed. Again, I did this with no assistance from either Jane or Lorena.

Shortly afterwards, Lorena had a vacation planned, so Jane was in charge. Only one payroll had been run with the new system. Lorena and Jane had several private meetings and discussions leading up to her vacation. None of the meetings and/or discussions were shared with me. The GOG was developed by them and/or someone else.

This time, which included a day Lorena took off for a funeral, was very stressful. Jane had noticed a position elsewhere for a payroll administer. She spent a significant amount of time going back and forth with a friend (the same one who had initially told me to email her if I had any questions) for assistance on updating her resume. They also had several discussions regarding the competencies for this position. During this time, I was processing and sending payroll and missed my coffee break. I was still sending payroll when they left for lunch.

Upon completion of sending payroll, it was well into the lunch hour. I went for a quick walk and returned to work on my course. When Jane returned, there were numerous questions on other job duties that were yet to be completed and if I had done them. While I tried to explain I was late leaving for my lunch, it did not seem to register.

When it was time to process the payroll during Lorena's absence, Jane slid her chair over to my computer and told me to do it. I followed the GOG exactly as it was written.

What neither of us realized was that some of the groups did not go through. We both left for a late lunch. When we returned, I noticed something different regarding the savings bonds deducted. Immediately, Jane told me I missed it. I stated I had not. After contacting the new software company, I found out a group of employees' payroll had not been sent. Unfortunately, it was past the banking institutions' deadline to have them sent. Jane ran out of the office in tears to Tonya. I am unsure if it was Jane or Tonya who alerted the city manager of the concern. While this was happening, I was speaking to both the financial institutions and the software company in an effort to rectify the situation. It took some time, but the problem was rectified and the employees were paid on time. The problem was a missed step in the GOG. This was also corrected.

As with another situation, I suspect I was blamed for the above error, as well as others. Another one, in particular, was when again the GOG was lacking. A group of employees was double paid as a result. We were provided a list and had the duty to collect from each of them. Some chose to come in and pay, while others wanted it taken off a future pay. Oddly, the list and details kept changing, and it was thus difficult to know who was and was not left to repay funds. I finally made a spreadsheet of my own and had all of the details within. It was shared in a shared file on the computer; plus, I kept a copy in my personal file. I continued to update both. While mine remained untouched and easier to see who was left to repay, the other one continued to be an issue. Jane refused to collect payments in person, yet she continued to involve herself in the details. The receipts collected, along with any information within the folder(s) often found themselves on her desk.

The new payroll program was additionally stressing to various departments and staff responsible for inputting shifts and differentials for each staff members. While most had the same training by the friend of Tonya, some were having difficulty understanding the complexities of how to input properly. One of them was an organization that was considered "at arm's length," or separate from the city.

Clerical staff responsible for the input of payroll details for their applicable staff were having difficulty comprehending the correct processes. As a result, I spent most of my lunch coaching the staff and the executive director in this area to better understand how to enter all of the necessary details. During this whole time, I was continually badgered in the background by Jane and Lorena doing so. They advised it was "their problem." I attempted to suggest that it was beneficial to them, as well as us, as helping educate any department would result in fewer errors for us to attempt to catch prior to payroll processing.

With the variety of changes, there were often future payroll changes that were to be filed according to pay dates. This had been an issue prior to my start, and therefore, whoever printed off the information sent to payroll by email was to colour code each one they printed and filed. Colour coding was also utilized in an effort to indicate who may/may not have been filing the changes into appropriately the applicable future pay dates. All three of us had the generic payroll email on our computers, as well as one of our own. At one point, I began to print two copies of each change. I would file each one as normal and then had a filing system in my drawer to follow up on. I caught a few that mysteriously disappeared the normal way.

One day, Loreana was upset over another missing change that was overlooked. Immediately, Jane went to her computer. I had a hunch she was looking to make sure it wasn't hers, and I went to look on the payroll email. While I was watching, I saw the error was Jane's. However, as I was looking at this email, she was attempting to change it to me, but was having difficulty. Jane then stated that it appeared to be both of us. That time, I called her on this. She initially denied it, until I stated that I'd seen her attempting to change it. Jane's response was, "Fine. I'll change it back." There was no remorse. And Lorena sat there, watching and listening, yet not a word was said to Jane. Lorena simply shrugged and looked away.

Still trying to process this act, along with everything culminating up to it, I drafted and emailed a letter to Lorena. Admittedly, it was lengthy and emotional. By that time, I had had enough. The emotions I was going through by that point were plentiful. What came next shocked me even more, however.

I was summoned to Tonya's on Monday. Upon entering her office, I saw that she had my letter on her screen. Immediately, I became uneasy. From there, I was asked how I thought Jane would feel if she knew what I had written about her. I couldn't believe it. It felt like Tonya was being condescending and ridiculing me. I don't recall my exact response, but her next response was to reframe her question and ask me how I would feel if Jane said what I did about her. My response was along the lines that I would never have behaved the ways she did, and that if I had done as she had, I would expect it.

The conversation continued with me questioning the appropriateness of Jane framing me for her mistake(s). Tonya responded by saying she wasn't going to tell me if Jane was written up as I was. To this, I replied that I was not asking. I already knew Jane had not been. I was then told I was "talking over her" and the discussion was over until *I* calmed down.

The following day, Tonya came into the office with a broken talking stick. This talking stick was utilized during meetings for everyone to be aware of whose turn it was to talk. She made a crack that it had been thrown or broken after someone was talking over her. Both Lorena and Jane found the joke very amusing.

From there, things escalated very rapidly. The following week was a pay processing week, was a shortened week due to a long weekend, and Jane was off on vacation. I chose to work again over my lunches, coffees, and after work to ensure everything was completed on time.

When I received my second ROD (Record of Discussion) in June 2016, Lorena asked me to go for a walk (in front Jane). I looked at both of them and asked if I was "in trouble." With the looks exchanged between the two, it was clear that both Lorena and Jane had knowledge of the upcoming discussion.

Just prior to this, my mother had passed away on Boxing Day of 2015, we had a house fire (January 2016), and dealing with insurance was by far more stressful than the fire itself. My husband, special needs daughter, and I had been living in a fifth-wheel camper in my husband's shop since the end of February. Just prior to the second ROD, I found out my father was ill and I was concerned that he might have cancer. I was very worried and stressed.

We discussed some of the errors, and I agreed I had made the mistakes and explained the situation. Lorena responded, "I have too much going on and can't be there for you." Then she told me, "You need to leave your personal problems at the door."

I acknowledged that yes, she was busy with preparing for the new payroll program and I certainly did not expect her to take away from that. When she asked if there was anything I needed, I asked if I could use one of my vacation days to take Friday so I could go see my father, who was approximately three hours away.

During the weekend, I thought about the ongoing problems I had been having with Jane. As Lorena had asked if there was "anything" she could do, I texted her to ask if I could perhaps meet and discuss some concerns with her. Lorena replied, "Sure." I drafted some of the concerns in anticipation of finally discussing some of my worries. After we discussed the ROD, she told me she had forwarded it to the Tonya and she would discuss it with me.

On Monday, Lorena waved the ROD in front of Jane and I and asked where we should meet to discuss it. I was shocked at her unprofessionalism. We met in the office beside the payroll office. I simply initialled it as any "excuses" were apparently not tolerated. However, there were a few points on the written ROD that I did not recall and about which I asked for clarification. Lorena said she couldn't elaborate, as Jane had advised her. I was yet again shocked. Yet again, I was deemed guilty simply by Janes say so, even after she was caught framing me.

Fast forward to the week after the September long weekend of 2016. Upon my arrival to work, I was presented with a large stack of ROEs Jane had failed to complete. They were late and could have then resulted in additional fees from the Canada Revenue Agency (CRA). Added to that was my requirement to complete the workload of myself and Jane's prior to payroll processing. Payroll processing started Wednesdays. This left me one day to do all of the work. Thankfully, I had stayed late the prior week in an effort to be prepared. I completed as much as I could prior to processing, with work leftover to be completed afterwards. With my pre-planning, along with working through numerous coffee breaks and staying late, I was able to complete the necessary work to ensure payroll was processed on time.

What I wasn't aware of was that Lorena was micro-analyzing every tiny mistake she could find over that week. At the end of this short week, and just as Lorena was ready to leave, she presented me with a written warning, then left abruptly. The work in process was part of the written warning. And, I was not only noted for my mistakes, but also for failing to catch Jane's errors. Despite this, I stayed about an hour and a half on my own time to finish up unfinished work and write a note as to what I had not finished of Jane's unfinished work and errors made by her.

Upon returning home, I shared my written discipline letter with my husband. We were both in disbelief. I was exhausted. It felt like I couldn't do enough or do anything right. Despite all of the extra hours, honesty, diligence, and attempts to rectify differences, it seemed I could only do wrong. I was devastated.

I ended up off on stress leave. I had to go to my nurse practitioner. As I was overly emotional, did not want anyone to see my tear-stained face, and was embarrassed over my inability to control my tears, I wore my prescription sunglasses to my appointment. While speaking to the nurse practitioner, along with another one in training, I had difficulty controlling my tears. I was provided anti-depressants, ensured I wasn't suicidal, ensured I was speaking to a counsellor, and advised to go back regularly.

One day, upon returning from one of my appointments with my nurse practitioner, I received an email demanding I undergo a functional abilities test. This was stipulated to be returned within days. I emailed to advise I would be unable to have this completed in the timeframe, and when I would be able to.

I went diligently to the counsellor through the employee assistance program (EAP). While he did not provide specifics, he acknowledged there seemed to be a problem within the organization, and he indicated that he had worked with a few employees.

The counsellor assisted me with a few techniques to help me. My mind kept replaying the events that had led up to this. It felt like I was in a constant fog. I avoided going out, not wanting to see anyone. I was ashamed, ashamed that this was the second time, and that despite attempting to hold on and be strong, I crumbled. The first time, I had walked away and grieved over a job I had loved. I just wanted to curl up a ball and hide from everyone and everything. I had nothing left to give. I felt like an empty shell. I had nothing left inside.

Sleeping was fitful. Pretty much every night, for two to three years, I was up for an hour or two. When I did sleep, I had frequent nightmares. Often, I would wake my husband and/or daughter by screaming in my sleep. While not as frequent, to this day, I continue to have nightmares during which I scream out in my sleep.

A discussion wherein I admittedly became upset and raised my voice resulted in the three of us having a meeting with Tonya. This was called a "mediation." During this meeting, Jane was called out on her lying by Tonya. All three of us were present. Jane made a few rude comments. During the meeting, Tonya suggested moving both of our desks so that Jane could not continually be hanging over my shoulder and worried as to what I was/was not doing. Afterwards, Jane and Lorena had a private meeting with Tonya after excusing me.

When I came into work early (as usual), I noticed Jane was in Tonya's office. Immediately, I felt uneasy.

The same day, Jane refused to move her desk. Tonya appeared to go along with this. With the cramped space, this meant I would have my desk in an awkward position. Regardless, I moved mine to attempt to have some personal space, even though we were only feet away from each other. This resulted in numerous comments from anyone trying to come into the office. It was not conducive to communicating with anyone coming into the office or within. As a result, I moved my desk back.

Shortly after the meeting/conciliation, there was a company barbeque. I had only been there just over a month. Lorena, Jane & I had all initially talked about going as a group and I was told it would be a great place to meet the rest of the staff. The day of the barbeque, Lorena and Jane gathered their stuff and simply asked if I was planning on going with them. I looked at them in shock and said I had thought that was planned.

As soon as we arrived, they bolted and made a point of ostracizing me. I visited and tried to make the best of the situation—feeling quite uncomfortable—and almost left to walk to the hospital as my mother was having a chemo treatment at that time. When it was time to leave, Lorena and Jane came out of the building and called out to tell me they were leaving. I was seriously looking at leaving and finding alternate work then.

The response from Lorena and Jane about their behaviour at the barbeque was:

"Because you told on us, we were mad at you."

"What did you expect? You got us in trouble."

"We were mad at you."

To make a long story a little shorter, the "investigation" took three or four months. Instead of addressing all of the information requested Elvira—only a portion of the documentation were included with the formal complaint was referred to. The rest was referred to as duplicate or "redundant." It was pieced apart and basically blamed me for everything. Stories were changed; Lorena, Jane and Tonya denied what they had previously acknowledged.

While dealing with Workplace Safety and Health, it appeared to have been basically refused to deal, along with this response. He cited that I had the legal route available, which I had also been dealing with at my own cost. I questioned him about the response and also requested a supervisor or manager review it as I was not in agreement. Approximately a week later, a different Workplace Safety and Health worker left a message for me.

I responded with an email:

Hello ____,

Could you please help me to understand the follow clips I copied off of the website (Workplace Health & Safety Act) of https://web2.gov.mb.ca/bills/38-4/b210e.php

My questions were noted.

Duties if harassment occurs

42.2(3) *An employer who knows or ought reasonably to know that workplace-related harassment is occurring must ensure that*

(a) the source of the harassment is identified and the harassment stopped; and

(b) adequate steps are taken to remedy the effects of the harassment.

As noted, they were aware—despite later changing their stories.

Referring a complaint to an officer

42.5(1) *A worker who reasonably believes that he or she has been subjected to workplace-related harassment may file a written complaint with a safety and health officer.*

I had included the safety & health officer in the initial complaints. He did not respond to any of the issues. Instead, ___ , the previous HR director (friend and previous direct supervisor to the new HR director), handled the "investigation."

42.5(5) *On receiving a complaint under subsection (1), a safety and health officer must promptly investigate to determine if workplace-related harassment has occurred*

Same as above.

Right to refuse work

42.6(1) *If a complaint of workplace-related harassment has been filed, a worker may, after giving notice to his or employer, refuse to work, if*

(a) the harassment substantially interferes with the worker's ability to perform his or her work and the worker reasonably believes the harassment will continue; or

(b) the worker's health or safety is jeopardized by continuing to work.

The doctor's notes & the "Return to Work" forms completed (as requested/required by HR Director) by my practitioner reflected the harassment issue within the department & inability to return unless this was addressed.

Worker to remain off-site

42.6(4) *Pending the investigation and determination of the safety and health officer, an employer shall not require a worker who refuses to work under this section to return to the workplace unless*

(a) the employer takes reasonable disciplinary action against, or provides harassment-prevention training to, the person or persons allegedly responsible for the harassment; or

(b) the employer makes reasonable alternative work arrangements for the worker to ensure the worker will have minimal contact with the person or persons allegedly responsible for the harassment.

Nothing was done—except to change stories & twist information around.

Note: This took approximately three months on the employer's end, despite the policy stating it would be 10 days.

Worker to be paid

42.6(5) *Until the matter is finally disposed of, a worker who does not return to the workplace under subsection (4) is deemed to be at work during the hours the worker would normally have worked, and the worker's employer must pay the worker for those hours at the regular or premium rate, whichever would otherwise apply.*

I have been without pay for the last several months—upon running out of "sick time" in September, then utilizing my overtime banked, and vacation time. And, this matter has NOT been disposed of. It is clear that the "investigation" is flawed in numerous ways.

Please help me to understand how an employer, who is aware of the problems—admits to issues within the department to me (as well as others) —but later denies & changes their stories in the "investigation," can do so without any questions or investigations by Health & Safety?

Are there further avenues, such as supervisors within Workplace Safety & Health, that this can be referred to?

Any assistance would be appreciated.

Thanks

xxxxx

Note: To this date, I have not received a response.

Do you have any suggestions/help you may be able to provide me with? Thanks

Despite being financially strained, my husband and I attempted to address this through a lawyer. We presented the lawyer with the information. He was initially shocked over the mishandling of the situation and wrote a letter to the city manager.

A note regarding the following letter:

- Reference is made to an email of the updated respectful workplace policy being sent to employees December 22, 2015.

My mother was in the process of passing away at the time and died four days later.

A few comments made previously by both Elvira and Tonya through my head. On more than one occasion, they laughed and commented on how they would often write letters for the city manager, which he would simply sign.

The term "disgruntled employee" was frequently utilized by both them.

Also noted are numerous other comments regarding me. Yet, not once did the City Manager speak to me to hear any of my concerns or hear my version of the events.

As far as I was aware, I had addressed my concerns as required, in verbal, emailed, and written form.

Following is a reproduction of the response:

Dear Sir:

Thank you for your letter on October 6, 2016 with respect to our employee, _____.

Contrary to Ms. _____'s assertation to you, the City's current Respectful Workplace Policy was adopted May 13, 2008 and was most recently amended December, 2015. You will note from the attached "City of _____ Policy Receipt Acknowledgement" that Ms. _____ did in fact receive a copy of the policy on April 30, 2015, as acknowledged by her signature. Additionally, all City employees with a City email account received the December 22, 2015 updated version, together with an email from _____ outlining the three revisions made at that time. Ms. _____ does have a City email account and did receive this email.

Ms. _____'s dedications to her position with the City has never been at issue. Her performance has had to be addressed during her employment and the latest incident occurred September 9, 2016, just prior to her medical leave. As I am sure you can appreciate, Payroll is an area requiring considerable attention to detail and Ms. _____ has not been giving it her due attention to ensure her work is accurate. She has been making careless mistakes that cannot be tolerated and when the City has attempted to address this with Ms. _____ her response has been to place blame on her co-worker, manager, and ultimately her employer. Expectations for improvement were set out for Ms. _____ and she will be held to these upon her return to work.

Ms. _____ had previously complained about her co-worker and it was determined that many of her complaints were unfounded and in fact appeared to be an attempt on her part to deflect responsibility for her own actions. Ms. _____ does not appear to understand the roles she plays in this relationship. Ms. _____, then Deputy Director of Human Resources, met individually with Ms. _____ to hear her concerns, and then conducted a mediation with both parties in an effort to address the concerns and arrive at some solutions to building a positive relationship between these co-workers. At the conclusion of this process, Ms. _____ herself agreed it was helpful.

I resent your implication that our City management team lack the skills and abilities to foster a collegial and competent workforce based on the complaints of one disgruntled employee. I am proud of the team we have at the City and appreciate all they do to ensure a healthy workplace for our employees.

You have urged we take steps to ensure our policies are fairly and consistently applied. I assure you this occurs on a regular basis. I would in turn urge that Ms. _____ follow established city policy and processes of which she has been made aware. At no time did Ms. _____ follow established City policy and processes of which she has been made aware. At no time did Ms. _____ file a Respectful Workplace complaint in accordance with the policy. Rather, she sent an email to our Safety and Health Officer, with copy to our then Director of HR, complaining about her co-worker and advising him that she had also sent an email citing harassment to the Human Rights Commission and Provincial Workplace Safety and Health Department. She then forwarded that email expressing her disappointment with the values/ethics within the department.

Ms. _____ has made her position known through every avenue other than the internal process that was available to her. It is my opinion there is nothing to be gained by a meeting.

Respectfully,

City Manager

Naturally, I was hurt and bewildered. I was shocked over the unflattering depiction of me, particularly from someone I had never once spoken to. As he was a person in a leadership position, I was bewildered over how he could garner any information about me without once speaking to me.

And I was puzzled over what appeared to be a lack of concern over the issues being raised by not just myself, but also by numerous other employees whom I would later meet and discover have suffered similar treatment. Some of these employees, I was later advised (by other former employees), had signed non-disclosure agreements.

At my husband and friend's suggestion, I attempted to have my concerns addressed through the ombudsman. Although they were sympathetic, I suspected my complaint would go nowhere. And that is exactly what happened.

Attempts to have my experiences addressed through the Minister were either ignored, or a response was received from an assistant. This response appeared to also be negatively judgmental toward me, without reaching out to me for details. With the state of mind I was in, I finally chose to give up.

I was diagnosed as having complex post-traumatic stress disorder (C-PTSD). The definition of this, according to Wikipedia, is:

> Complex post-traumatic stress disorder (C-PTSD; also known as complex trauma disorder) is a psychological

disorder thought to occur as a result of repetitive, prolonged trauma involving sustained abuse or abandonment by a caregiver or other interpersonal relationships with an uneven power dynamic. (Complex post-traumatic stress disorder, 2021)

While I received a package to apply for long-term disability (LTD), I failed to complete it until just before it was due. I intended on filling it out, yet with my state of mind, I kept deferring it. I saw and knew of various cases (including case laws) whereby victims of bullying were refused LTD and subjected to further scrutiny. I didn't feel that I was well enough to have to answer the numerous comments and scrutiny I feared I would be asked by the LTD provider.

When I attempted to contact the LTD provider, it was either the day before or the day the forms were due. I knew I should have completed them and had them in previously, yet I was still struggling with the feared scrutiny.

I understood the questioning as to why I had not completed them earlier. As the LTD provider's representative asked further questions about why I had not contacted them earlier, I fought back tears and attempted to explain the situation to her. I was still mad at myself for not having my emotions under control.

The person I spoke to advised she would call me back either by the end of the day or the following workday. That never happened. When I called again, I was simply told I was too late.

I was further upset with myself for failing to complete the forms and submit them within the timeframe required. My state of mind was still a mess.

Months later, I received a letter via email and registered snail mail advising that I was being laid off.

Finding employment afterwards was a challenge. At one point, I kept a spreadsheet of the positions I was applying for. I had the suspicion that some of my applications were being hampered due to my previous employment.

Not only did I finish my payroll compliance practitioner (PCP), but I also finished my education in human resources. I took online courses and obtained my university certificate in human resources/labour relations (UCHRLR). As well, I travelled for approximately 11 hours to take a workplace investigation course. After that, I took courses on mediation and completed my certificate in that.

Taking training in investigations and mediation further entrenched my belief that both the mediation and poorly conducted investigation were far from proper. But, at this point, I was attempting to move on by seeking employment elsewhere.

I sent an application to a business owner who had previously advised me to contact him should I be interested in employment. He owned a business within the same small-town-like city. The position was what some might consider lower from my previous position. His assistant advised me that he would contact me. I never heard back regarding the position.

There were a few amazing opportunities I had applied for. The interviews had gone well, and I was advised they would be checking references. The references provided knew my work ethics and abilities. Plus, I had continued with my education.

Yet, upon checking with them, they had not been contacted. And, when I attempted to contact the interviewers and human resource personnel, I did not hear back.

In another position for which I applied, I personally handed a resume and application to the new executive director for an agency. This new director was the former executive director of the group I had spent some of my own time to assist in educating about the new payroll program and inputting employee payroll. While at the time she was very appreciative, her reaction to my application surprised my husband and myself—her sneer and eye rolling were quite noticeable.

There were numerous other applications to which little to no response was received.

Finally, in February 2021, I was offered a position after attending an interview the previous evening. The wage initially offered was less than I had been making six years previous and prior to my certifications. While nervous, I did manage to negotiate closer to where I had left off in my hourly rate; however, I would not be eligible for benefits for close to a year.

While excited by the opportunity and ability to finally provide for my family, I was (and still am) wary of the possibility of further workplace harassment and bullying. I am constantly attempting to analyze and watch for any signs of potential toxicity within my workplace.

I am enjoying the new role and challenge. I have signed up to take further courses toward another certification for this position. Yet, I fear daily that they may change their minds, fear trusting my co-workers, and fear that things will happen as they did before.

I am pushing myself to pick up quickly. Again, I am making myself a training manual so I can refer to it currently and in the future. Anytime I make a mistake, I am upset with myself, even more so than before my employment with the city.

And, as I am working in the same general area of municipal government, I am worried this story and book itself may jeopardize my employment.

My fear of losing this position has me detaching or attempting to detach myself from enjoying it. Yet, I know I would be very upset if it actually happened. I fear writing this experience may also jeopardize my employment. Numerous questions roll around in my head as I write this. These questions all circle the concern and fear over the "what ifs" of this experience and how they may attempt to end this new opportunity for myself and my family.

My special needs daughter is also terrified, partly due to her strong attachment to me and her fear of changes. She has enjoyed having mom home the last several years. She has me see her off to her day program and welcome her home each afternoon. But I hadn't realized her fear of my being bullied in the workplace again.

Besides the changes in routine, my daughter frequently asks for reassurance that I will not tolerate being bullied as I was before. She continually asks if I will be sure to walk away if similar behaviours arise. She is scared that I will end up at the point I was before—a complete mess, with the inability to sleep more than a few hours at a time, up most of the night, fighting tears, and in a constant state of fog.

I feel terrible that my daughter had to witness the disintegration of her mother and her mental health. It made me realize that the experience affected not just me, but also my family, and greater than I had realized.

I am enjoying the job, the challenge, co-workers, and everything and anyone surrounding it. And I sincerely hope this story does not affect it negatively.

Section 2
Culture

Figure 8.1: Cartoon by Cathy Cox

"The culture of any organization is shaped by the worst behavior the leader is willing to tolerate."

—Steve Gruenther and Todd Whitaker,
School Culture Rewired (2015)

CHAPTER 8:
The Role of Corporate Culture in Workplace Bullying & Harassment

Defining workplace harassment and bullying is just the beginning of where one can begin to learn about workplace bullying and harassment.

There are other mitigating factors that enable, contribute to, and increase the probabilities of occurrences of harassment and/or bullying within the workplace.

One of the biggest (if not the biggest) factors contributing to, encouraging, and permitting bullying is the organization's culture. Workplace culture, like a person, develops and similarly morphs according to the beliefs, values, behaviours, actions, attitudes, atmosphere, perceptions, and so on of those within.

Much like anyone, the culture or personality of the organization is vital—it is the heart of the organization. It is the centre, the heartbeat of the given organization, as seen in Fig. 8.2 Every action surrounding it directly attributes to and/or affects the culture.

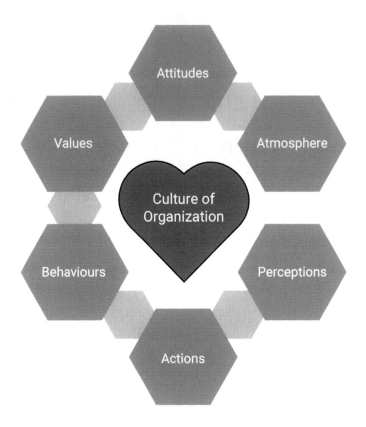

Figure 8.2: Elements of organizational culture.

The culture of an organization directly contributes to the prevalence of bullying and/or harassment, and whether it is or is not accepted. If it is allowed in any shape or form (regardless of rank or position), it will thrive and flourish, quickly becoming a pandemic within.

Basically, the organization takes on a persona of its own and its activities, behaviours, beliefs, actions, assumptions, values, atmospheres, actions, and so on are observed by those within. Like children watching and learning from their parents, employees observe and perceive the actions and behaviours of others within as acceptable or unacceptable. Whether a behaviour is acceptable or unacceptable is determined by the actions and behaviours of those tolerated and allowed in leadership positions, as well as any other position within.

The organization's personality further develops the values and beliefs of those within. It affects how those within dress, act, and even perform in their positions. This becomes the organizational culture.

Organizational culture includes whether poor behaviours (and more) are tolerated or dealt with and handled appropriately. Unhealthy cultures tend to foster negative attitudes, perceptions, actions, values, behaviours, and atmospheres. Some of this includes bullying tactics and behaviours, as noted earlier.

CHAPTER 9:
Ignored Behaviour is Condoned Behaviour

With our current pandemic ongoing, Christmas 2020 was a notable time.

Federal public health guidelines indicated Canadians were to avoid all non-essential travel outside of Canada. Some provinces (i.e., Manitoba, Alberta) restricted and/or banned gatherings, including Christmas. Yet, various political figures were later caught travelling during the pandemic (Somos, 2021).

These politicians have presumably not suffered the loss of income that many others have. Numerous small businesses were forced to close. There were temporary and permanent job losses, temporary and permanent closures of businesses, and temporary or permanent reduction in hours and/or income as a result. And, while there were some government programs providing subsidies or income, not everyone was able to benefit.

Hearing of those in leadership positions going on vacations abroad would not have been so upsetting had they not been preaching the importance of the strict lockdown measures. This is similar to those in leadership positions emailing and touting zero tolerance toward workplace harassment and bullying. It gives the appearance that it is okay for some, but not others. It erodes any trust people might have had for those in leadership positions not following their own preaching.

Watching the actions of these politicians does not encourage others to follow the public health orders. Understandably, there was significant feedback following these revelations, and the added possibility and risk of many choosing to do the same and/or choosing to ignore restrictions, such as banned gatherings. Take, for example, one of numerous articles on politicians travelling despite lockdowns and travel restrictions:

'Stupidity': Experts slam politicians' travel amid coronavirus pandemic - National | Globalnews.ca

The above scenario is comparable to the stated expectations of some organizations. While they state they are "zero tolerance" and have respectful workplace policies, their actions and reactions portray otherwise. Regardless of the organization, they need to be proactive and "walk the talk." More than positive quotes, emails, and assurances (or emails of the applicable policies) are needed. Every organization needs to provide ongoing, consistent training on respectful workplaces. Follow-up and follow-through on all situations (reported or not) is essential.

Understandably, there are a number of employers who are frustrated and tired. Many organizations have become leaner throughout the years. Managers/supervisors/and anyone in a leadership position is tired. Many have now become responsible for extra duties, sometimes with little or no further training on such things as respectful workplaces. It is not surprising that some in leadership positions become frustrated and feel the employees complaining are "disgruntled" or "unhappy" people.

That is another important point on why this book has come to be. I, along with numerous others I have interviewed, have dealt with this more than once. While other forms of abuse are not the same, it is interesting how there appears to be a number of those who have suffered workplace bullying in more than one workplace.

I will not get into the cycle of abuse here, but it is common thread I have noticed with a variety of those I have interviewed. And, as a result, it is another speculation about those who deal with the wrath of workplace harassment and/or bullying.

Questions about those who bully versus those who are bullied come to mind. There are a number of questions for both bullies and those targeted. What characteristics do either have? How far is either willing to go? How about their upbringings? Behaviours? There is an abundance of questions anyone can delve into, but this is one area this book simply does not have the space to address.

However, one area that can be explored is the actions (good or bad) of those within leadership positions.

The following example provides a glimpse of poor judgment by a city manager, a top bureaucrat (Barghout & Levasseur, 2019a; Barghout & Levasseur, 2019b).

There were several online articles regarding Rod Sage and Christine Mitchell. Rod Sage was the City Manager/CAO for the City of Brandon, Manitoba. He was also a non-voting member on the police board.

Christine lived at Rod Sage's house for five years prior to her death from an overdose in his home.

According to one article, police were unaware of the overdose until almost two days after her death. Fluid samples were discarded by the hospital, and no autopsy was completed. It was a member of the public who apparently reported her death to the police.

Subsequent articles provided further information. Neighbours interviewed noted the frequency of police presence at the house. Discarded needles were found in the neighbourhood. People were coming and going at all hours from Rod Sage's home.

A quick internet search provides an abundance of news articles on this story. While these stories prove some concerning details regarding Rod Sage and Christine Mitchell, they also raise an abundance of concerns and issues regarding this. Just how much was the city aware of? Were there background checks done prior to Sage obtaining his position with the city? If they were aware, what, if anything, was done? How and why was he allowed to continue on the police board, regardless of whether his position was non-voting? Why did it take so long for him to resign from the board? Would every other employee be provided the same treatment given similar circumstances (i.e., paid while off for several months)? What kind of perception does this portray to employees within? What do the taxpayers perceive?

When behaviour such as this is ignored by any employer, it is viewed as condoned. With this example, not only did at least one city councillor support this employee, but the mayor did as well. Employees watch and take note of what happens and how situations are handled. As a result, aggressive behaviour (including bullying) that is ignored is also regarded as acceptable.

Lapse(s) in judgment, lack of morals, or any poor behaviour tolerated leads others to believe it is condoned and/or accepted. This is whether the behaviour is that of the general public or employees.

If it is seen as acceptable for someone in a leadership position to have lapses in their judgment, many employees throughout any given organization see this as acceptable behaviour. After all, if the mayor and at least one councillor are defending Sage, then similar behaviour should be acceptable from them.

As another saying goes:
"Ignored behaviour is condoned behaviour."
—Author Unknown

This is regardless of its mission and goals, values, or emails stated on behalf of the organization.

Is your organization doing all that it can to promote a safe and respectful workplace? Why?

As most of us are aware, actions speak louder than words. Posting plaques or signs (on missions, goals, or values of the organization) on the walls is nice. Sending out emails encouraging a respectful workplace is also nice. But more needs to be done to encourage and enforce respectful workplaces. Everyone within the organization needs to be able to recognize and understand the importance of a healthy workplace environment.

The ability to recognize and understand the importance of culture within is vital for any organization. Creating and maintaining a positive culture in any organization takes a committed effort for all, and it includes everyone—top-down, bottom-up, and everyone in between. As Dr. David Yamada states, in his article titled "Workplace Bullying and Ethical Leadership,"

> It starts at the top. Organizational leaders must send a message that workplace bullying is unacceptable behavior. Executives and managers who preach and practice dignity will see that quality resonate throughout an organization. Establishing a culture of open, honest, and mutually respectful communication will have the salutary effect of reducing bullying and other forms of employee mistreatment. (Yamada, 2008)

Some tout their mottoes, slogans, policies, and such to be their culture. They may be very passionate about the organizations in which they work, and about how they hire the right fit for their organization. But do they really understand what that is? Is it the culture of the organization? Are they aware of how they and/or the organization is perceived from the outside in? Do they really know and understand the culture within? Would they and those in leadership positions recognize toxicity within?

Many, if not most of us, have heard about how some organizations hire the right fit. This is in reference to an employee fitting into their culture/company. But do all companies fully understand the culture of their organization? Is the image of what they perceive the same as that perceived by everyone else within? How about those outside the organization, such as prospective employees?

Sometimes the organization's culture is not as healthy as those in leadership positions or others within may believe. Or, perhaps some within are aware of failings, but fail to consider how these may impact their ability to attract more talent.

Many prospective employees are savvy enough to do their own homework regarding prospective employers. This is a key item some employers fail to consider.

Social media (i.e., Facebook, LinkedIn) is part of the research process a prospective employee may utilize, as it is for some employers. Some employees notice the frequency of job postings (particularly the same ones) that show up from prospective employers, which indicates high turnover. High turnover can suggest a toxic culture. Prospective employees inquire with current and former employees and with various contacts regarding the specific business, and ratings and comments about employers can be viewed online.

Besides the culture of an organization, current and prospective employees also concern themselves with the leadership styles of those in leadership positions.

CHAPTER 10:
Leadership Styles

The term leadership appears to be a commonly and loosely used word. It seems many equate the term with positions. A position may be considered a leadership one, but that does not necessarily mean each person is actually a leader. A title does not make a person a leader, contrary to what some in those positions believe.

Part of the way an organization behaves has to do with the style of organization, or, more simply put, organizational theory. What does the company model? What kind of leadership styles do its leaders model?

Leadership styles also play an important part in how organizations are run. As a result, this also influences the actions and reactions of everyone within a given organization.

This is why I feel it is necessary to include brief descriptions, along with the pros and cons, of the more predominant leadership styles.

Autocratic

This leadership style is also known as totalitarian, dictatorship, or military. Autocratic leadership is a management style wherein one person controls all the decisions and takes very little input from other group members (Definition of "autocratic leadership", n.d.).

Many can relate to this older and well-known style. Employees are told what to do and how to do it. For many, the first examples that come to mind are Adolph Hitler or Kim Jong-un.

Some key points to keep in mind about this style are the following. The leader makes the decisions and authority is primarily in the hands of one person. There is little to no input from staff and rigid rules.

Pitfalls of this type of leadership include poor morale and decreased productivity. It often results in distrust, may result in higher absenteeism, and may also result in higher turnover, with often the best/better employees departing. Autocratic leadership can be a default style for those who are insecure or underqualified in a leadership position.

Manufacturing, military, and construction can be a good fit for autocratic leadership. Pros of this type of leadership include:

- Decisions are normally made quickly.
- There is a clear chain of command.
- Rigid rules (i.e., safety and occupational) can prevent injuries in dangerous occupations.

Bureaucratic

This type of leadership is defined as "a system for controlling or managing a country, company, or organization that is operated by a large number of officials employed to follow rules carefully" (Bureaucracy, 2021). Bureaucracy is primarily used in the public sector and is popular in governments (all levels) and health authorities.

Keys to this leadership style include focus on the administrative needs of the organization and a preference for consistency, standardized processes, and numerous policies and procedures, along with rigid rules and regulations.

Bureaucracy can have pitfalls, however. It can be inefficient due to excess paperwork and red tape. It may have excess rules and regulations, may limit creativity, and is generally inflexible to change. Bureaucracy may also promote the presumption among employees that time served within the organization equates with the right to promotion over others.

This can be problematic if there are newer staff that are more experienced, educated, and capable staff.

This leadership style is prone to promoting employees and managers until they reach a position of incompetence (Peter principle), where they remain until they retire or die. A final pitfall of this leadership style is that some people in leadership positions within bureaucracies may be more autocratic than bureaucratic. Sometimes this may be due to inexperience, need for further education and/or training, or insecurities.

Bureaucratic leadership has its pros, too. In bureaucracies, roles and responsibilities are normally more clearly defined than under other leadership styles. In addition, bureaucracy theoretically ensures (or at least promotes) a fairer and more equal system, which is contributed to by the processes, policies, regulations, and rules involved. This leadership style promotes safety and a safer environment and is thus a good choice for food (handling, preparation, cleaning, packaging, and distribution) and safety (clothing, footwear, regulations, and much more).

Democratic

The democratic leadership style is also known as participative. Democratic leadership balances decision-making responsibility between the group and the leader. Democratic leaders actively participate in discussions, but also make sure to listen to the views of others (Carlin, 2018).

An example of a democratic leader is Sir Winston Churchill.

Under this leadership style, everyone has the ability and/or opportunity to participate. Creativity and collaboration are encouraged, and the knowledge and abilities of each member are valued. Other key points include the fact that the leader maintains the final decision; however, power is distributed.

Pitfalls of this leadership style include situations with a lack of communication that can result in unfinished projects, and waiting for input by others in the team takes additional time and often results in further delays. Resentment, along with fewer people sharing ideas, can result when suggestions and/or ideas are consistently taken from a select few. This style of leadership may lead to employees' uncertainty or concern over the capabilities of the person in the leadership position; for example, this may occur when a supervisor delays decisions in order to consult team members even when decisions are time sensitive.

A few pros for democratic leadership include more varied viewpoints, increased morale and job satisfaction, and encouragement of creativity and honesty.

Delegative

Also known as laissez-faire, free-rein, or a hands-off approach, the delegative leadership style is a method that assesses the unique talents of each employee and assigns responsibilities accordingly (Laissez-faire leadership: Definition, tips and examples, 2021).

With delegative leadership, as the term suggests, work is delegated and tasks are shared. Examples of leaders who use this style include Steve Jobs and Warren Buffet.

This is the least intrusive of the leadership styles. In this style, the leader delegates work and, while two or more employees are provided decision-making powers, the leader remains responsible for the decisions. Employees are trusted to complete their tasks.

Unfortunately, this leadership style can be the least productive and may lead employees to question if the person in the leadership position cares. Other pitfalls include the potential for confusion in roles, and employees being free to make their own decisions. Thus, confusion may happen when employees are looking for input and direction, and they may not know who to approach.

If implemented properly, delegative leadership can promote greater workplace satisfaction. The abilities of each individual are utilized to enhance the organization. Employees are given the resources (information and training, for example) needed to complete their duties. And, when they request input or advice from leadership, they are supported.

While employees are expected to solve their own problems, those in leadership are available to provide guidance when needed.

Strategic

The strategic style of leadership "refers to a manager's potential to express a strategic vision for the organization, or a part of the organization, and to motivate and persuade others to acquire that vision. Strategic leadership can also be defined as utilizing strategy in the management of employees" (Juneja, 2021). Wayne Gretzky, Tony Blair, Lee Iacocca, and Steven Spielberg are all examples of strategic leaders.

This style of leadership is also described as "a practice in which executives, using different styles of management, develop a vision for their organization that enables it to adapt to or remain competitive in a changing economic and technological climate. Strategic leaders are able to use this vision to motivate employees and departments, fostering among them a sense of unity and direction in order to implement change within their organization" (Sales & Holak, 2021).

One of the key points of strategic leaders is that they will often utilize reward or incentive programs and aim for efficiency. Strategic leaders encourage and embrace varying viewpoints, keep updated with trends and changes, encourage questions, and promote collaboration. Users of this leadership style view mistakes as an opportunity for learning and encourage an open and transparent culture of positivity.

Pitfalls of strategic leadership include that it is complex and time-consuming. It can be difficult to implement, and few are able to achieve effective use of this leadership style due to its complexity.

The most obvious pro regarding strategic leadership is financial. If it is skillfully implemented, the organization identifies and investigates potential opportunities. And, as a result, they are able to identify the strengths and weaknesses of their competitors.

Coaching

This leadership style, sometimes referred to as performance coaching, is characterized by collaboration, support, and guidance. Coaching leaders are focused on bringing out the best in their teams by guiding them through goals and obstacles (Lee, 2020).

An example of a leader who used the coaching leadership style is Mahatma Gandhi, who said, "You must be the change you wish to see in the world," and, "In a gentle way, you can shake the world."

The key to this style of leadership is that the leader quite literally coaches or guides their employees. Learning and training are continuous. In this mentoring style of leadership, the leader encourages people to believe in themselves and their abilities.

However, this style does have its pitfalls. It can be time-consuming, and it is difficult for many in leadership positions to achieve or execute. It takes long-term commitment, and few in leadership positions have the skills and/or expertise necessary for the coaching style of leadership.

Pros for coaching leadership include encouraging better communication, constructive feedback, being supportive in place of judgmental, and increased support for personal and professional development.

Visionary

"Visionary leadership has been defined as the ability to create and articulate clear visions providing meaning and purpose to the work of an organization (Nanus, 1992; Sashkin, 1992). Visionary leaders develop their own personal vision then merge it into a shared vision with their colleagues." (Taylor, Cornelius, & Colvin, 2014)

Examples of leaders who have used this leadership style are George Washington and Oprah Winfrey. This type of leadership is normally utilized when an organization is being transformed and/or during times that are challenging.

Key points about this leadership style include that these leaders can be described as inspiring, innovative, strategic, focused, optimistic, emotionally intelligent, bold, organized, imaginative, and enthusiastic. These leaders have a vision as to what an organization can become, and they look to the future. Leaders who use this style can have very infectious drive and enthusiasm. They have the ability to predict change in business trends, both positive and negative.

Pitfalls of this type of leadership style include too much focus on the future. These leaders may fail to address pressing problems or situations in the present. Tunnel vision may occur, and the leader could fail to consider other details necessary for success. If other leaders within the organization are not in line with the visionary style, it is difficult to execute.

Servant

The servant leadership style is often referred to as a participative or socially responsible leadership style.

> The servant-leader is servant first ... It begins with the natural feeling that one wants to serve, to serve first. Then conscious choice brings one to aspire to lead. (What is servant leadership?, 2021)

Leaders who have used this style include Abraham Lincoln, Martin Luther King, and Nelson Mandela.

The essential element to this leadership style is that its main goal is to serve others. This is referred to as the servant-first concept, where the servant is the employee. Leaders who use this style consider employees' needs first, and the organization looks to contribute.

Common pitfalls of this style of leadership include that it can lead to role confusion between leader and employee, and that it is a long-term commitment that takes time to implement. True servant leaders are few and are difficult to find. There are strong possibilities of loss of motivation and productivity. In addition, servant leaders may have difficulty providing honest and constructive feedback on employee performance.

On the flip side, decisions made in an organization whose leaders use servant leadership are made in the best interest of the organization. This contributes to increased trust, teamwork, and inclusion. As a result, employee loyalty and commitment can also be higher.

What happens if and when those in leadership positions fail to portray essential skills? How about poor behaviour left addressed? Ensuring the missions and values of any organization are followed consistently? This means that *all* employees (top-down, bottom-up, plus everywhere in between) are aware of and following them.

Have you heard or seen the saying, "With great power comes great responsibility"? This is otherwise known as the Peter Parker principle, from the Spiderman comics. People who are in leadership positions are given huge responsibilities. One of those responsibilities is overseeing employees.

Failure to make an ongoing effort to ensure a positive environment leaves room and opportunity for the growth of negative culture within any organization. Just like the coronavirus, toxic corporate cultures can flourish if provided the opportunity or "right" environment.

Whether or not it is realized, the behaviour of anyone in a leadership position is noticed. Employees (as well as peers) may model their behaviour as it is seen as acceptable. Disrespectful behaviour toward anyone is also picked up on. Employees being harassed or bullied are further harassed by others following accepted behaviours and actions. Like a virus, it festers and grows.

CHAPTER 11:
Examples of Poor Leadership

The following are a few examples of poor leadership, some of which I have personally viewed and experienced.

1. Assuming the Sick Aren't Sick

Key here is the assumption that a person on medical, disability, or sick leave is playing the system, and/or their doctor(s) signing the note is aiding this. Always assume the employee is sick.

Regardless of the leave, it should not be questioned. As with most (if not all) leaves, sick notes are signed by doctors or practitioners. These professionals are not in the habit of simply signing employees' time off for no reason.

It has been (and still is) shocking at the amount of those in leadership positions who automatically assume an employee is playing the system.

It is acknowledged that there may be some who do play the system. The data and information I have seen (both in work and preparing this book) suggests they appear to be a minority. Yet, as with so many other areas in life, this can cause additional hurdles for those who are legitimate. Perhaps this may be, in part, due to the employer's inability to visualize the illness or disability.

Sometimes a power struggle begins as a result. While the employee is off on medical leave, they are sometimes made to then jump through hoops. This can include frequent requests for updates, additional paperwork, monitoring via co-workers or leadership, and so on.

Understandably, an employer needs to continue to be updated and aware of a possible return to work. They need to ensure proper coverage for the person who is off. Vacation or days off for those within the same department and surrounding it need to be provided and planned for. Training and education for both the person filling in, as well as co-workers, are another consideration, and there are also the budgeting aspects surrounding the person's position.

Then there are additional costs associated with having an employee off. While a temporary employee can fill in during the interim, there can be a variety of additional costs. Advertising, recruiting, and hiring (even within), along with training (whether on the job or otherwise) are all added costs. And it is often more difficult to find staff for temporary work.

Regardless of whether warranted or not, frustrations build. Those with poor leadership qualities can, and often do, attempt to expose cases that are actually genuine, causing further undue stress when mental health is involved. Unfortunately, I have worked alongside some in leadership positions who have noted their frequent, if not automatic, assumption of employees abusing the system by obtaining sick notes.

Yes, there are employees who are "frequent flyers," as some in leadership positions have commented. This was a common perception from some of those in leadership positions in healthcare where I previously worked.

One of these positions included scheduling, where I have had a few people actually admit to manipulating the system to their benefit. Usually, it was calling in sick to have a day off with pay. I can also recall a situation where one employee went off on WCB, yet a few co-workers noted the injury resulted off the job while gardening.

While there are some that can and do cheat the system, not everyone does. From my experience, there are more who do not seek to cheat the system than do. Assuming one or all are doing so is something that should never be done.

The article by Stuart Rudnar, titled "Don't rush to judge employees on medical, disability leave" (included in the appendix section), signifies the importance of this.

2. Requesting a Functional Abilities Form and Then Not Following It

Another example of poor leadership is requesting that an employee complete functional abilities forms for stress (mental health) leave(s) and the leader then failing to follow up on the form, address the comments on the form, implement the form's suggestions, or follow the restrictions on the form.

Functional abilities forms have a variety of areas to complete pertaining to an employee's *abilities* and/or restrictions. While some organizations take in the physical versus mental-health-related problems, not all have progressed toward the ability or understanding of the differences.

Some of the particulars that are commonly requested on a functional ability form may include:

- Standing
- Sitting
- Lifting from floor to waist
- Lifting from waist to shoulder
- Stair climbing

The functional abilities form initially began as a tool to aid in return-to-work programs. These forms were intended to assist in a smoother transition for those injured at work.

Utilized properly, they can be effective for all parties toward the transition back to work. All parties (employer, union, WCB, employee) can benefit by working together.

Unfortunately, there are some organizations that routinely utilize these forms as a tool to intimidate the employee back to work or, as noted earlier, expose what is thought to be an employee abusing the system. Functional abilities forms may be another tactic to push the employee into returning too soon and/or to encourage the affected individual to resign.

Whether the forms are completed for someone internally or externally (i.e., Workers' Compensation, an insurance company, or a return-to-work facilitator), these forms are often utilized. Their advantage is that they can help all involved (employee, employer, insurance, etc.) to better understand the capabilities and limitations of the employee. By being aware of the employee's abilities, the employer can then better understand the adjustments needed within the workplace, and the employee can also better understand their limitations. With that, a return-to-work program can be developed to help all involved.

Some employers have adjusted the form(s) to include further abilities, such as:

- Concentration
- Judgment
- Memory
- Public contact

Included in most, if not all, functional abilities form(s) is a section for adding further details or comments on abilities and/or restrictions. These comments provide another opportunity for employers to ensure a safe workplace, physically and mentally.

As an example, and to add further clarification, I will continue with the previous example of my own experience.

After attempting to remain strong and trying to weather the unhealthy work environment, my mind and body had finally had enough.

I exhibited a number of physical and mental characteristics. I was exhausted yet unable to sleep through the night. Having previously had few stomach ailments, I was now on medication for stomach upset/indigestion. My concentration was limited, and headaches and body aches were common. By the time I ended up at my practitioner's office, I was a mess. With my shame, humiliation, embarrassment, and fear of anyone seeing me a mess from fits of uncontrollable crying, I wore my sunglasses even in the practitioner's waiting room and office as I waited to see her. Long afterwards, my practitioner and I would joke about this. I was fortunate to have a supportive, knowledgeable, and understanding practitioner. Like most in whom I finally confided, she was shocked at the workplace environment and culture.

When I returned home from one of my regular appointments, I received an email with a functional abilities form attached. The letter stated it was to be completed and submitted within *days*! Naturally, this added to my stress and anxiety, which were already through the roof.

Upon contacting my practitioner's office again, I was instructed to advise my workplace of my inability to have it completed until my next appointment.

At my next appointment, I presented the form to my nurse practitioner. Some of the additional details noted by my practitioner included:

> No problems with public contact but contact with some employees may cause undo stress, impacting ability to complete tasks/concentrate/and affect judgement. This includes, but may not be limited to employees within the department.

And the response to, "Is there anything the employer can do to assist the patient in an earlier return to work?" was "Modify work environment- address work environment issues within the department."

Despite this, nothing was done or offered by my workplace, except to ask when or if I would be returning.

3. Failing to Follow Policies

This seems like a no-brainer. A worthy leader should not need to be told the significance of following their own policies, especially respectful workplace (harassment or bullying) policies. Yet, it is astounding the number who will circumvent or avoid following their own policies. Presumably, this is for a wide range of reasons.

As an employee, I have seen a variety of cases, for others as well as myself. Both myself and numerous others to whom I have spoken have experienced the lack of proper and full follow-through of workplace policies.

In the case study in chapter 7, pretty much everything within the policy was not followed. The investigation had not only been requested via email, but had to be pushed by a formal letter as well. Despite the policy noting the employee was to be paid during the course of the investigation, once my sick bank, vacation, and overtime was drained, I was without pay.

Later, having further educated myself, I realized how poorly the investigation was executed.

While I was an employee under the HR umbrella, the HR director was the investigator. As far as I was aware, she had little to no training regarding workplace investigations. And, she was aware of both my husband's and my concerns regarding the possibilities of her bias and conflicting interests during the investigation process.

Documentation provided included:

- Various dates and times of concerns/situations between myself and my co-worker.
- Actions against myself, which included:
  - My co-worker demanding assistance from me, yet refusing to assist when I needed assistance. This was frequent and often occurred with the supervisor present and aware of what was happening.
  - Providing false information and/or procedures.
  - Icing and ignoring me.
  - Ignoring/trying to isolate me from group activities.
  - Blaming me for mistakes I had not made.
- Soliciting others to participate in bullying behaviour, most notably the person in the supervisory position. Eye rolling, exclusion from information and training, and icing me out were just a few examples.
- Catching my co-worker in the act of framing me, with the supervisor again present and aware.

Not surprisingly, the outcome was chalked up to "she said/she said" and was said to be inconclusive. This was yet another insult to the injury.

It still astounds me as to the lengths and degrees some people in power positions will go to avoid following their own policies or win, in their eyes. One notable case is *Boucher v Wal-Mart*, which is discussed in chapter 12.

In reality, everyone loses. The person in the leadership position loses respect. The company loses the respect of their employees. Morale suffers. Employees not directly affected may reconsider their loyalty to the company. As word spreads, turnover will likely increase, along with recruiting costs.

Whether unionized or non-unionized, and regardless of the policy, it is imperative that all members of the organization follow the organization's policies.

4. Avoiding/Ignoring/Discounting Glaring Leadership Issues

Avoiding, ignoring, and/or discounting glaring leadership issues can include:

- Performance expectations or appraisals for employees but leaders are exempted.
- Failure to address a lack of or need for leadership skills in a person(s) in a leadership position.
- Poor leadership skills or a lack of skills required in a leadership position.
- Lack of accountability.

Regardless of any position, no one is perfect. We all make mistakes, and we can all benefit from feedback and encouragement. Further education and training can and should be provided for everyone.

Is everyone within living up to expectations? Are they following the values stated by the organization? Or are the rules and/or expectations bent for some? Are these guidelines haphazardly followed? Are a select few exempted from them? Is there any favouritism? Are friends in leadership positions exempt? Is there nepotism? Has there been a need for nondisclosures? In cases of a board of directors, are they simply going along with those in charge, or are they ensuring the culture is a positive one?

An important yet often overlooked responsibility is the poor behaviour of a boss (whether CEO, city manager, CAO, executive director, etc.). Are their duties and responsibilities clear? Do they have expectations and does someone follow up/through on whether they are being followed? Who do they report to? Is there a board of directors? Are deficiencies in skills/behaviour addressed? Are there consequences for poor behaviour? In the case of municipalities and cities, are the councillors responsible? Are those overseeing them aware of their responsibilities and how to fulfill them? Are there conflicts of interest?

As listed previously, there could be a myriad of reasons for problematic behaviour and/or a lack of essential skills. These can include negativity, poor communication, lack of integrity or honesty, insecurity, arrogance, nepotism, self-serving behaviour, and more.

There is also the Peter principle (as noted previously), which is common in the bureaucratic leadership styles.

If there is a need for additional training (*and* the person is willing, able, and trainable), then training needs to be provided. Yet, all too often, this appears to be missed. Sometimes it is simply a lack of follow-up by whoever (i.e., manager, supervisor, director, councillor, whoever the person in the leadership position reports to) should be cognizant of any deficiencies.

Performance appraisals can aid in indicating areas of improvement for any employee. This may include the need for further education and/or training. Unacceptable behaviour that needs addressing is another concern. Performance appraisals should be completed properly on all employees, regardless of their position.

Just one additional note on *properly completed* performance appraisals: writing your own appraisal or increase in salary/benefits letter is not appropriate and should not be considered properly completed. This is another shocking thing, but it was admitted to at one of my prior workplaces. At this particular workplace, a few in leadership positions actually admitted on more than one occasion to writing their own appraisals or letters recommending an increase to their salary or wages. What was even more shocking was the signature authorizing this by of the person they were purported to be reporting to.

A performance appraisal should be an opportunity to address any areas of deficiencies, as well as acknowledge the positive aspects of an employee's work. Leadership can highlight and encourage necessary or beneficial training, if needed. Discussions on what can be done to improve should be considered, and it is important to provide guidance and encouragement toward improvement. Regardless of who we are and how much education we may have, there is always room for improvement. Plus, highlighting employee's positive attributes can and should be done.

We have all seen situations where a person in a leadership position is unable to deal with conflict, address bullying situations, and/or is lacking a myriad of other skills needed for the given position(s). The case study in chapter 7 provides several examples of this. Sometimes leaders could benefit from further training, yet they and/or the person they report to fail to address what is lacking.

Excuses often appear as:

- "But they are a good _____."
- "They bring in a lot of revenue."
- "That's *Bob's* son."
- "They didn't mean to _____."
- "They are just a little rough around the edges."
- "Staff should know better."
- "They get results."
- "They are the one in _____ (leadership position)."
- "How dare the employee tell on him/her."

- "What right does the employee think they have to tell _____ how right/wrong a procedure is/is not."

Comments like those above are concerning. These give the perception that employees have little to no right to question those in leadership. Employees are beneath those in leadership positions. As such, they are expected to do as they are told.

There may be a suggestion(s) that employees are their "subordinates" and they are "lower" than the superior in rank. As well, it may be implied they are in no position to complain or suggest they are being unfairly treated, particularly by their superior. In fact, when referring to a letter regarding workplace bullying/harassment by a manager, a new manager angrily stated, "*You* pissed them off."

Sometimes, nepotism also comes into play with a failure to address leadership issues. Nepotism can be described as favouritism toward ***relatives*** or ***personal*** friends by those in ***power***. Because of their ***relationship*** rather than their abilities, these people receive special treatment (e.g., *jobs*, discounts) (Nepotism, 2021).

In my previous workplaces, I have experienced situations where superiors socially intermingle with those who directly report to them. Whether platonic or otherwise, the resulting lack of objectivity can pose problems. The case study in chapter 7 provides some examples of this. Numerous questions about friendships or relationships such as these can be raised. Some of them include:

- Is it appropriate?
- How are any appraisals conducted?
- Are they done fairly as any other employees?
- Are deficiencies in how they conduct themselves addressed?
- Are any/all complaints addressed fairly and adequately?
- Who ensures the fairness and integrity of all of those in leadership positions? The higher the position, the more delicate this can be.

Regardless of position or rank, all employees should be provided with critique and feedback, positive and negative. And *everyone* should be aware of their duties and requirements regarding workplace harassment and bullying, regardless of their position, rank, or relationship.

Avoiding, ignoring, or discounting glaring leadership issues and/or improperly conducting appraisals based on a position breed distrust, erode loyalty, and destroy morale.

5. Tagging Employees

Tagging involves alerting other departments within an organization to an undesirable candidate. Although this can happen within a variety of large organizations, the example I am referring to occurred in another place of employment.

This other place of employment also was known to follow the bureaucratic leadership style. There were numerous other satellite "offices" elsewhere within the province, as well as departments within each them. They included several different unions. As a result, there are many processes and guidelines, which may include recruitment, retention, application for positions for internal and external candidates, as well as term positions.

I would frequently hear numerous employees comment on internal applicants being tagged. Until I actually witnessed and experienced it, I was skeptical.

I would never have believed it had I not seen it for myself. Sure, I had suspected it. In fact, numerous co-workers suggested that I had to have been tagged. I had stellar performance reviews, ongoing coursework and training at my own initiative and cost, was advised on numerous occasions of my efficiency, attention to detail, and ability to multitask, and more. Yet, numerous internal positions I applied for and was fully qualified for didn't even provide me an interview.

At another person's suggestion, I made an appointment to speak directly to the HR director to see if she would provide feedback. Was it my resume? Were there courses or training she might recommend? When we met, I asked if she had any recommendations or suggestions that might help me in achieving an interview or position. I was stunned and in disbelief when there were a few less than professional remarks. The subject was then changed.

Coincidence or not, the next position (a term) I applied for, I received an interview. Shortly afterwards, I started this position. It was in this position where my suspicions were confirmed.

This position meant working directly with another director, along with additional responsibilities and duties. Some of this included reference checks and dealing directly with applicants for a particular department. While it was a demanding position, I enjoyed it (and everything and everyone within it) immensely.

What disturbed me was actually seeing bright tags stapled to some of the applicants. These tags indicated that one was to contact the HR director (at the time) prior to contacting those "selected" applicant(s) involved.

Problems? Several of the particular applicants were knowledgeable and good employees, the tags were outside the union contract, and the primary concerns of the HR director appeared to be personality conflict(s) or difference of opinion with someone in a leadership position.

In my opinion, employees were tagged as a result of speaking out against unethical or bullying behaviours.

There were numerous employees, including myself, who attempted to speak out against bullying behaviours. This was not received well. The following point (number six) is one example of what happened to both myself and another co-worker I had worked with.

Tagging people limits advancement opportunities and can ultimately trigger the tagged person to eventually leave. This is often the intention or desire of the person in the leadership position. While this might perhaps be the goal of the person in the leadership position, the departure of the employee is just the tip of the iceberg.

Similar to poor customer service, poor treatment of employees spreads quickly. Like those in leadership positions, employees talk. Both within HR and outside the department, the employee faces further ridicule and bullying despite attempts to address the behaviour and be respectful.

Tolerating behaviour such as this allows the perception (from all of those within) that it is acceptable for all (co-workers, supervisors, managers, and directors) to treat given employees poorly. As a child learns, so does anyone within a given organization—they watch and learn what is accepted. And, when permitted, these behaviours reflect negatively on the organization as a whole.

Affected employees often depart as a result. They, along with co-workers, friends, and family, also notice. Other co-workers may depart. Morale goes down. People outside the organization become aware of the actions and behaviours of those inside the organization.

Potential candidates who have experienced bullying and/or harassment are acutely aware of toxic organizations. As a result, they are more selective toward the organizations to which they will apply. For myself, this is regardless of the need for a job—obtaining a position in a healthier organization is more important than employment in another toxic organization.

Companies perceived to be toxic will often receive fewer applicants. A number of bullied comrades with whom I have spoken can attest to this. As a result of bullying experiences, former employees such as myself (and the numerous others interviewed) conduct their own reference checks into potential employers. The Workplace Bullying Institute, other sources, resources, and word of mouth all indicate more difficulties for toxic organizations in recruiting and retaining skilled employees.

Recruitment and retention costs then increase. With some positions that require additional education and/or skills, this can then require the added costs of perhaps:

- Additional on-the-job training
- Company-paid education
- Increased recruitment costs to attract employees

Any position of authority holds great responsibility and should not be taken haphazardly or lightly. Concerns or complaints regarding any employee (in *any* position, top-down, bottom-up, and anywhere in between) should be verified. If verified, any issues or problems should be dealt with directly, fairly, properly, and professionally.

6. Leaders Advising Employees to Provide Negative Feedback on a Co-worker

Confused?

This is another personal experience, and also experienced by other co-workers. Numerous attempts were made to address workplace bullying issues by a person in a supervisory position.

The primary concern raised: a facility supervisor appeared to target given employees, along with exhibiting a variety of tactics employed by bullies in the workplace.

Numerous departing employees all cited the same problem: the same supervisor.

Soon, I began to have the same concerns. It began with little comments here and there. Then, guidelines would change. My workload continued to increase substantially. During this time, another co-worker would frequently be reading novels, casually chatting on the telephone, or in the supervisor's office. Despite approaching both this supervisor and the area manager, my workload continued to increase. I would frequently cover for the other four within the office, sometimes more than one of them at a time. My duties ranged from scheduling, typing out meeting minutes, records duties, and front desk, financial, and other duties. In an effort to do better, I would often come in earlier and sometimes leave a little later. But no matter how much work I completed or how well, things continued to deteriorate.

Another employee, also having difficulty with the supervisor, took a different approach. She openly disagreed with the supervisor against a variety of tactics employed. A particular concern was the refusal of overtime if it was not approved prior by the supervisor. Whether it was overtime or otherwise, this employee would confront the supervisor with her concerns.

Sometimes this employee could also be demanding, without realizing or understanding the workload the office was under. Some of us, including myself, would become frustrated over what appeared to be the expectation that we should be of dropping other work to complete work requested by the department this employee worked. Everyone's stress level was escalating.

At one point, all of us in this office were directed of "our duty to email anything negative regarding this co-worker" to management. This direction came from our area manager, who oversaw our location, supervisor, and a few other locations. We were to email *her* manager of anything. I suspect most of us imagined (or, at least hoped) that they were working to improve the environment for the better.

We were shocked when this particular employee emerged after another meeting between those in leadership positions. She informed us she had resigned. She gave me, along with others a goodbye hug. I sat in shock, disbelief, disappointment, and guilt.

Days later, we were all informed of policies and procedures regarding speaking to the press. It was clear we were not to speak to anyone, particularly the press. Doing so could result in loss of employment. We all adhered to the directions. None of us wanted to risk our employment as we knew we were all lucky to have jobs we liked that were well-paying with benefits.

While I definitely loved my job and the majority of people I worked with, I secretly felt justification and relief when a few co-workers openly voiced to me that they saw how poorly I was being treated. I was relieved that it was not just in my head. My concerns and complaints were warranted.

Around this time, I had a co-worker desperately wanting time off for a family function. However, there were already the maximum number of people off or away on vacation. It was a Friday, which was often busy. This would have meant me covering my position, the two others off, and hers.

The area manager suggested closing a department two hours earlier, as it had been done for special circumstances. I agreed that it was a good idea. However, the supervisor convinced the area manager to have the person who would normally be done at two in the afternoon stay on overtime.

When this co-worker's normal shift was over, she had agreed to work two hours of overtime to cover scheduling. Both she and the supervisor spent over an hour in her office with the door closed. When they emerged, they presented me with the additional job of attempting to fill shift. I am certain my face relayed confusion and shock. I was perplexed at why I was presented with this duty when this was the sole reason she had stayed late with overtime.

Despite this, I attempted to fill the shift. I mistakenly thought she would at least answer the switchboard should it ring while I was making calls. However, instead of doing so, she made calls for sponsorships for a car derby and casually visited with those called. At one point, I did call out, asking if she was going to answer a line.

By the end of that day, I was beyond frustrated. I had also dealt with a variety of the supervisor's and this co-worker's other tactics. Besides downloading some of her work, she had also spread false information to a few other previous co-workers. Some of this information included false accusations and claims about what I said about them.

I eventually resigned but did note my concerns within my resignation letter. This letter included concerns, such as:

- The feeling of no other choice but to leave
- Toxic environment
- Disrespectful workplace policies
- Lack of trust

Instead of addressing the concerns raised, the manager then advised a select group of employees of their *obligation* to forward any negative feedback on me as well.

To me, an authentic leader does not require or advise the employees of the requirement to provide any and all negative feedback they can on a co-worker.

This leadership is clearly unethical. These behaviours can have numerous ramifications, including legal ones. Tactics such as these show who people in these leadership positions really care about: themselves.

Regardless of the position of the bully, the person targeted continues to suffer their wrath, particularly when the person doing the bullying is in an influential position.

Future prospective employers requesting references from these businesses (i.e., references from recent/most recent work experience) become a challenge, even when/if they provide the employee the opportunity to advise why this may or may not be an issue. More often than not, regardless of whether or not the potential employee is upfront about the previous employment, the employment opportunity is lost.

Authentic leaders care about their team. They have values and principles like honesty, ethics, and morals. Authentic leaders are willing and able to admit deficiencies in their capabilities, along with taking steps (i.e., training) to address their inadequacies. They provide open and honest communication, with no gossip. They strive to have a psychologically safe workplace.

Bullies in higher positions frequently network with a variety of people in numerous positions and capacities. This can happen at work functions (in the case of cities, there are numerous functions held, often including numerous managements, some staff, various business leaders, politicians, etc. in attendance at each), educational seminars, groups (i.e., Chartered Professionals in HR [CPHR]), or at business and personal functions (company picnics, hockey games, etc.). Unfortunately, there are a few in leadership positions who utilize these connections unethically.

Connections forged via a variety of the channels noted are sometimes utilized to further themselves, and to the detriment of others. While it is hopefully rare, there are situations where bullies in leadership positions continue to wreak havoc on the lives of employees they have bullied. And who would most of the connections believe? In my experience, as well as those of others I have interviewed or to whom I have spoken, it is normally the one in the leadership position.

While some of these organizations have policies or standards denouncing this, few are prepared to be the whistleblower on workplace bullying or unethical behaviour.

7. Constructive Dismissal

Failure to address concerns made by staff, including concerns raised in resignation letters and exit interviews, can increase the instance of toxic environments.

First of all, in the previous example, my resignation should *not* have been accepted. A skilled manager and/or HR professional would know and understand what constructive dismissal looks like. Part of the education requirements for a human resource professional are learning and understanding the implications of constructive dismissal.

My letter clearly stated my feelings of having no other choice but to leave, outlined the toxic workplace, and detailed the respectful workplace policy. All of this points to constructive dismissal.

Another excellent example of constructive dismissal is Boucher v Wal-Mart, discussed in chapter 12.

As constructive dismissal is a big topic, it's addressed in detail in chapter 16.

8. Negligent Hiring and/or Retention

Like constructive dismissal, *negligent* is another legal term. But I feel it is less confusing to understand.

Most of us understand the term negligent. Alternate terminology of negligent may include careless, neglectful, lax, lazy, remiss, and irresponsible. In other words, someone was careless or failed regarding their responsibility.

When we add the terms hiring or retention, it is obvious it is regarding employment. Employers need to show their due diligence when it comes to hiring and retaining employees. This is particularly when they knew, ought to have known, or became aware of concerns regarding potential employees or existing employees.

Negligent Hiring

An example of negligent hiring could be in a situation of sexual harassment in the workplace.

Sometimes employees hired may have had a reputation or a record regarding abusive behaviour, bullying, and/or sexual harassment. If the hiring employer has failed to exercise due diligence in the hiring process, they may be subject to negligent hiring.

There are a variety of background checks that can be completed, depending on where one lives. Information may include:

- Driving infractions or suspensions (for couriers or semi drivers)
- Criminal record check
- Vulnerable sector check
- Child abuse registry
- Drug testing
- Physical exams
- Incarcerations
- Parental leave

Are there gaps in the potential employee's resume? If so, can they be explained reasonably?

Keep in mind, however, gaps may also indicate taking further schooling, inability to find employment, family responsibilities, or being self-employed.

Have references been verified?

Have qualifications, including certificates or diplomas, been verified?

While most potential employees are honest, I know of situations where fake certificates have been utilized. Obtaining official transcripts, as well as contacting the applicable post-secondary institution, may be beneficial.

What about background checks?

Has the employee or prospective employee provided details on their departure from previous employment? Is it reasonable and necessary to contact the previous employers? Are prospective employers aware of potential legislation regarding privacy legislation on reference checks for given areas?

Note that in some extreme bullying and harassment cases (e.g., Meredith Boucher in *Boucher v Wal-Mart*), some employees have difficulties finding employment afterwards.

While there are many who contact previous places of employment, I also urge the importance of ensuring the information is fair and objective. There are a number of additional avenues to further verify information about potential employees.

Speaking to references the potential employee provides is the first step. Even if references are not previous employers, they may hold significant information regarding their integrity, honesty, ethics, and work habits. Previous co-workers are also excellent sources and may provide further insight on a potential employee's work history. They may also elaborate on reasons for their departure, including whether they may have dealt with bullying or harassment or other reasons.

If the potential employee does not have a recent previous employer, give them the opportunity to provide an explanation. Be open and understanding. As a person who was bullied, I have also left employment due to expectations of improper bookwork practices. Employers who are known for a lack of integrity and/or bullying are often known elsewhere for their culture.

Often, ratings on almost any organization can be found by doing a search on the internet. Employees and/or customers provide feedback and ratings regarding organizations and/or employers. Reading up on employee satisfaction and employee comments are just a few ideas. A few known online sites are Indeed and Glassdoor. In addition to that are social networking sites.

LinkedIn is one social networking site. Professionals will often have skills and endorsements by other professionals. Posts shared and comments made provide details on their beliefs, values, and interests. These also provide further details on other professionals they know and are connected with.

As with desirable and less-than-desirable employees, the same can hold for employers. More and more, there are examples whereby persons in leadership positions are overstepping their boundaries both while employees are employed at the given organization and afterwards.

Retaining a less-than-desirable employee is and can be risky. Issues may include sexual harassment, bullying, dishonesty, and violence. The #METOO movement has exposed numerous situations of organizations that were aware or should have been aware of situations such as this.

As with due diligence of hiring and retention, ensure the facts are verifiable and accurate from all. And, as a reputable, ethical, and fair organization, obtaining permission prior to reference checking is the right thing to do.

Not only is it morally and ethically the right thing to do, but it may also be legislated. For example, in some areas, there is privacy legislation pertaining to the collection, use, disclosure, and retention of personal information. This may include reference checks.

Negligent Retention

Negligent retention is a type of employment claim in which a worker claims that their employer failed to terminate or discharge an employee who should have been released from the company. In most cases, this involves situations where the employer knew or should have known that the worker in question had a tendency to commit:

- *Workplace harassment*
- *Workplace violence*
- *Sexual harassment*
- *Office bullying*
- Fraud, dishonesty, or other questionable types of conduct (Rivera, 2018)

The most prominent cases we frequently hear about are situations of sexual harassment. Harvey Weinstein is one of the most famous cases whereby negligent retention was claimed (Neumeister, 2018).

9. Conducting Reference Checks Without Consent

Reputable organizations will ask for permission prior to contacting references. This permission is normally a written request. Or they may request the applicant sign a form at an interview, providing permission to contact the references listed.

Occasionally, the job posting will stipulate to include references, with or without the request of previous/recent employers.

However, I have personally known some (including those I have interviewed) who have had prior employers contacted without consent.

A reputable organization looking for a valuable employee will at least attempt to be unbiased and neutral regarding previous employment. An employee may have left an employer due to a number of reasons that are favourable and/or admirable. I know several who have done so, including myself. There are valid and admirable reasons for employees to leave previous employers. Unethical business practices are just one of many. Naturally, these organizations would not provide the same response(s) as I (or others) would, should they be contacted.

Therefore, it is prudent to not only request written permission, but also keep an open mind should a potential candidate not provide a favourable response to contacting a prior employer. Give the candidate the opportunity to elaborate or explain their reason(s) for not contacting their previous employer. There may be valid and understandable reasons.

Backdoor references, such as calling/speaking to previous employers or co-workers not listed as references is not a practice most reputable organizations do. If your organization follows this practice, it might be worthwhile to reconsider, or at least question why. There may be valid reasons someone chooses not to list a previous employer as a reference. Bullying or harassment is just one of them.

As noted above, there could have been a toxic environment. Give the potential candidate the opportunity to provide feedback or their side to any negative feedback. Ensure that one-sided gossip is not taken as gospel.

There are both good and bad employees and employers. Those who fail to be objective can also fail to see the potential of some exceptional candidates.

Screening anyone out based on hearsay mirrors a follower instead of a leader. It is shocking the number of persons in leadership positions who listen to one-sided rumours from within and outside of their organization.

One excellent example is again the *Boucher v Wal-Mart* case.

10. Gossip and Exclusion of Potential Candidates

Gossiping about potential candidates and the exclusion of potential candidates as a result of slander or gossip should not take place. This pertains to all employees, regardless of position or rank, top to bottom.

Dana Wilkie's article, "Workplace gossip: What crosses the line?" (n.d.) provides important information regarding this.

Another article that I found insightful is titled: "Business of life: Stop complaining about your colleagues" (Riegel, 2018), which can be found on the *Harvard Business Review* website. This article points out the importance of normalizing feedback, whether it is positive or negative. It encourages calling gossip for what it is. And it promotes the value of providing feedback on a regular basis, rather than saving it for performance reviews.

One point they do not make, however, is when those in leadership positions gossip outside of the organization with other persons in leadership positions. This can tarnish the reputation of the employee(s) being discussed, as well as limit their potential future opportunities.

As noted, there are a number of reasons for everyone to avoid gossip within *and* outside of the workplace. Employers and employees are well aware that this frequently happens. Both have a choice of whether to believe gossip and/or rumours. A follower listens to gossip and fails to consider its negative consequences. Regardless of whether it is within the workplace and/or shared elsewhere (e.g., luncheons, networking events, social events, etc.), the results can be and often are the same. Gossip, if left to fester, can wreak havoc. Misunderstandings occur, at a minimum. Reputations can be falsely damaged, and often gossip can affect morale, personal well-being, and careers. The culture of organizations can and do suffer.

After Meredith Boucher left her employment with Wal-Mart, she had a significant amount of difficulty finding employment. One of the businesses where she stopped to drop off a resume noticed her name and made the connection with a comment regarding herself and Wal-Mart.

11. HR Leaders Indicate Lack of Opportunities

Here, HR leaders may threaten, suggest, indicate, or promote the lack of opportunities (both within the organization and elsewhere) that may result upon any employee attempting to address a variety of toxicity within the organization, particularly with someone in a leadership position.

A fair and ethical leader would not consider this, yet for a variety of reasons, some will. Unfortunately, this actually happens more than many may suspect or realize.

I, as well as others within a healthcare setting, attempted to address our experiences and concerns regarding a person in a supervisory position. Unfortunately, nothing was addressed. We, along with several others, ended up resigning.

Upon resigning, I also stated my concerns within my resignation letter. These concerns noted the large exodus of staff and further details. Unfortunately, this was not looked upon favourably.

Years later, I was again working in healthcare in another facility. As with my other position, I loved my job and the people I worked with. My performance appraisal reflected this.

However, I mistakenly trusted and confided in a manager. From then on, things spiraled downwards again. And, his exact words were, "*You pissed them off!*" It wasn't long afterward that I eventually left healthcare for good. The doors for any position, it seemed, had slammed shut. It did not matter how much education, experience, training, or excellent performance reviews I had.

Leaders' failure to verify word of mouth information provided to them is poor practice for a number of reasons:

- Legalities
- Ethics
- Lessens the pool of candidates
- Potential loss of skilled employee(s)
- Reduced respect of company and further erosion of its culture
- Further erosion of the company's reputation via word of mouth by unfairly judged candidates
- Added difficulty attracting skilled candidates

With the risks of legal action, it is simply astounding that an HR person would even consider following poor human resource practices.

Yet, it does happen. I have seen and heard numerous situations of just that.

Most, if not all, human resource certifying or affiliated bodies have codes of conduct against this very behaviour. Although most of these affiliated bodies encourage and promote the reporting of such behaviour, I would speculate the odds of people doing so would be low.

Why? One word is a significant contributor: whistleblower.

What Is a Whistleblower?

A whistleblower is an employee who reports or makes a complaint regarding a wrongdoing. Or, as the legal definition notes:

> The disclosure by a person, usually an employee in a government agency or private enterprise, to the public or to those in authority, of mismanagement, corruption, illegality, or some other wrong doing. (Whistleblowing, n.d.)

It can be regarding misconduct (e.g., fraud, health and safety, hostile workplace).

An excellent example (case law) is *Boucher v Wal-Mart*, discussed in further detail in chapter 12. An interviewer from CBC did an excellent job interviewing Meredith Boucher (Roumeliotis, 2014). This case really hit home for myself, along with others who experienced similar situations.

Meredith spoke on a number of problems she experienced being bullied. When she refused to follow her supervisor's direction, which went against her honesty and integrity, she suffered retaliation.

While whistleblowers show great strength and courage for what they do, too often they (as Meredith Boucher was) are targeted (retaliated against) after doing so.

As a result, not only does this affect the whistleblower, but it also affects anyone around witnessing. The whistleblower faces increased and often escalating toxic behaviour. Their mental health continues to be battered. And, if anyone even considers backing the whistleblower, the treatment toward the whistleblower convinces them otherwise. It is every person for themselves, as Heather Ilkin notes in her article included in the appendix, "We are hard wired to avoid threatening situations" (n.d.). Accordingly, I feel it is appropriate to include retaliation.

12. Retaliation

Retaliation in the workplace is more common than many people realize and includes the targeting of whistleblowers.

Both employers and employees may instigate and/or suffer from retaliation. It occurs as a response from the person(s) committing the bullying behaviour. It often arises as a result of their bullying behaviour being exposed. When questioned on the behaviour, there is, or can be, justification for their behaviour. (Chapter 2 explains DARVO further.)

Signs of retaliation may include:

- Exclusion. This can include meetings, training, information, office events (e.g., workplace barbeque, parties)
- Hostility, giving someone the cold shoulder, ignoring
- Bullying and/or escalation of bullying or harassment
- Delaying or blocking of advancement
- Reduction in pay (can also be construed as constructive dismissal)
- Discipline – Unfair, unjust, and/or unequal expectations
    - e.g., Same department, same errors made, yet only one person subjected to disciplinary action(s)
    - Sudden and/or increase in performance management (may be escalated and/or done out of normal procedure or order)
- Termination
- Post employment retaliation
    - Negative reference
    - No reference
    - Bad mouthing
    - Gossip
    - Sabotage of further prospects

With the above retaliation tactics that can (and again, too often) occur, it is no surprise as to how and why those around tend to simply be bystanders. As the appendix article titled "The bystander effect" notes, "The bystander effect can occur as a result of this desire to avoid harm, whilst also being able to rationalise the decision not to intervene by diffusing responsibility to others" (Ikin, n.d.).

Too often, I have seen cases where employees are ridiculed, shamed, and discussed within (and outside) organizations for attempting to address situations and/or assist a co-worker. This is yet another reason that bystanders fail to step up and back co-workers being bullied.

Yet again, one of my popular references is *Boucher v Wal-Mart*. As someone who has dealt with bullying workplaces myself, there are and were a few justifications from bystanders for failing to say or do anything. For a better understanding of some experiences from employees, please see chapter 12.

13. Poorly Conducted / Sham Workplace Investigations

Dr. Namie's (2008) statistics on workplace investigations provide startling figures:

> 1.7% conducted a fair investigation and protected the target with punitive measures against the bully.

> Yet

> 31% conducted an inadequate/unfair investigation with no punitive measures for the bully, but plenty for the target.

Shocking figures. And, while these figures are older, trends and statistics elsewhere suggest the current figures may be even worse. The City of Edmonton has been highlighted in the news for a few years. Despite promising to address the ongoing bullying and harassment issues, the October 2020 article "This is clearly problematic" denotes survey results on how most of the City of Edmonton's employees are not speaking out against inappropriate behaviour or discrimination (Cook, "This is clearly problematic": Most City of Edmonton employees not speaking up about discrimination or inappropriate behaviour, workplace survey highlights, 2020b).

Rubin Tomlinson LLP provides another interesting article regarding botched workplace investigations, entitled "B.C. bank botches investigation" (Rubin, 2014). In this situation, it was an employee working at a bank whose investigation was poorly conducted.

Notable case law on this topic that has garnered media attention is *Lalonde v Sena Solid Waste* and *Elgert v Home Hardware*. More details on these cases follow in chapter 12.

A useful article, included in the appendix, is Nathaniel Marshall's "A quick guide for conducting workplace investigations" (2019). Marshall provides basic, yet often missed, essential, and insightful guidelines many organizations seem to fail to address when it comes to workplace investigations. This is another suggested read for any organization unsure of where to begin.

In addition to the above-noted article, the Association of Workplace Investigators (AWI) has a wealth of information on workplace investigations. Further information on AWI is discussed later in chapter 18.

14. Lack of Confidentiality

Confidentiality should be a given. Toxic cultures and/or people seem to struggle with this. This can include gossiping, allowing rumours to flourish, persons in authority failing to follow codes of conduct, and failing to preserve confidentiality within and/or outside of the organization.

Some other areas where confidentiality may be lacking include disciplinary actions, possible or pending workforce reduction(s), employee sickness or disability, and workplace investigations. These are just a few of the topics that should only be discussed on a need-to-know basis.

As noted in the article "Confidentiality Breach Can Be Just Cause for Termination" (Saint-Cyr & Moradi, 2018), "The disclosure of sensitive employee and management information can also lead to a loss of employee trust, confidence and loyalty. This will almost always result in a loss of productivity."

With the above case, Ms. Manak was a client services manager with WorkSafe BC. Plus, she held the position of ethics adviser and oversaw claims for employees of WorkSafe BC.

As a person in her position, Manak was well aware of the confidentiality standards within WorkSafe BC. There were allegations of breach of confidentiality, including:

- disclosing details surrounding the termination of two employees prior to their termination.
- discussing information regarding the claims of two employees.
- disclosing that a staff claimant had threatened to report the handling of his unresolved claim to Global TV when his claim was disallowed ("I shouldn't be telling you this, but...": Court rules sharing confidential information is just cause for termination, 2018).

Failing to keep highly confidential information confidential destroys trust and is unprofessional. Confidentiality is essential for a person in a position of trust and authority.

15. Defamation of Previous Employee

Defamation from a person in an influential position of power can cause significant damage to a person's career and ability to find future employment. Yet, there are still those who attempt to do so. Take, for example, the case of *Musgrave v Levesque Securities Inc (2000)*.

Mr. Musgrave's previous supervisor implied to former clients of Musgrave that he may have misappropriated funds. Musgrave was an investment dealer with an excellent reputation. On top of the implication suggested, a prospective employer was advised that Musgrave was under investigation. What the previous supervisor failed to include was that this investigation had been determined to be groundless.

Musgrave sued. The supervisor was found guilty of defamation. As a result, Musgrave was awarded twice the notice period, as well as punitive damages.

I would love to believe this is an isolated incident. Unfortunately, it is not. Not only have I experienced this, but so have others I spoke to and interviewed in the course of preparing to write this book.

Many employees who have experienced defamation do not take legal action. Most simply do not have the financial means to do so. If they have recently left a toxic environment, they may be mentally unprepared to deal with it and/or unwell.

Regardless, any employer with integrity will not defame prior employees. Defamation is unprofessional. It reflects poorly on any organization, as well as anyone in a leadership position. Employees' reputations and careers (such as Mr. Musgrave's) are often damaged as a result. And their ability to find new employment may also be hampered.

16. Refusing to Provide Reference / Providing Negative Reference

Providing a reference is not a legal requirement in Canada. However, if the refusal to provide a reference is found to be in bad faith, the affected employee may be entitled to aggravated or punitive damages.

For example, in *Gillman v Saan Stores Ltd*, Mr. Gillman had been employed with Saan stores for approximately 32 years (1992). He was terminated after breaching company policy. Allegedly, Gillman had not only assisted with an employee in taking sick time, but also had the employee babysit for him. Upon management being notified by another employee regarding this, Gillman was terminated.

After his termination, Gillman applied for numerous positions. He advised family and friends of his job search and applied for jobs advertised in the newspaper. He had several interviews, with some resulting in a second or third interview.

After several months, Gillman was offered a position pending a reference check. Unfortunately, a few days later, the offer was rescinded due to a bad reference.

As a result of his difficulty in finding employment, Gillman hired an employment firm to assist him. The cost of doing so was over three thousand dollars.

Gillman later sought legal counsel and sued Saan.

Another notable case pertaining to providing a negative reference is *Trask v Terra Nova Motors Ltd* (1995).

In this case, Carl Trask had been employed with Terra Nova Motors for seven years prior to being falsely accused of theft.

Further to the accusation of theft, Trask's previous employer then advised potential employers of their accusation. This increased the inability and length of time to find future employment. His mental health suffered as a result.

Trask was later awarded $31,210 in damages. This included 18 months salary and damages for mental distress/aggravated damages.

As noted within the Canadian Legal Information Institute (CanLII) details:

> Thus, the manner of dismissal is not usually relevant; that is, unless it may be deemed to be a factor likely to bear on the employee's chances of obtaining another job. That is the situation here. The appellant not only mistakenly and improperly fired the respondent for the offence of theft and which of itself would have adversely affected the respondent's likelihood of obtaining and/ or retaining other employment, but it subsequently compounded that result by the highly prejudicial act of informing other car dealers (and perhaps others) of its reasons for terminating the respondent's employment. (Trask v Terra Nova Motors Ltd, 1995)

17. Improper Use of Progressive Discipline

Lack of knowledge and understanding by those in leadership positions often leads to poor responses to an employee's improper behaviour. These poor responses can include poorly executed progressive discipline.

Most employers are aware of the basics of progressive discipline. Simply put, the steps are:

1. Verbal warning

2. Written warning

3. Demotion, suspension, or performance improvement plan (PIP)

4. Termination

Progressive discipline needs to be properly administered, which includes following the processes in the appropriate order. As well, progressive discipline needs to be carried out in a fair and consistent manner. This means the person in the leadership position treats all employees equally and fairly. Otherwise, it may appear one or more employees are being targeted.

An example of improper use of progressive discipline is *Dawson v FAG Bearing Ltd (2008)*. Points I found of interest within the case cited include:

> In my view, FAG acted unfairly in the manner in which it terminated Dawson's employment. As I have indicated previously, FAG applied the Progressive Discipline Policy inconsistently when dealing with Dawson with respect to her third and fourth Discipline Notices and Gushue and Bauer in not issuing them a third and second Discipline Notice respectively with respect to the problem involving the hit marks. FAG failed to follow its own Discipline Policy by failing to conduct any independent and objective review of Dawson's suspension and dismissal. FAG was both unfair and insensitive in failing to investigate the reasons why, after almost 14 years of employment, and only after being transferred into a new position, Dawson suddenly began to experience quality problems. A fair and reasonable employer should be expected to investigate the cause of the problem and to attempt to assist the employee to improve her performance rather than march inexorably and resolutely towards dismissal. (Dawson v FAG Bearings Ltd., 2008, p. 49)

The discussion goes on to note that FAG failed to treat Dawson fairly, sensitively, and in accordance with their own policies.

Please refer to chapter 14 for more details on progressive discipline.

CHAPTER 12:
Bullying and Harassment Cases

When organizations fail to address workplace harassment and/or bullying at any level of an organization, it can escalate. This can often result in media attention and/or litigation.

Following are several cases pertaining to Canadian workplaces. As case law, they are decisions made from court cases and tribunals.

These cases are often utilized as examples for subsequent cases brought forward.

Boucher v Wal-Mart Canada Corp., 2014 ONCA 419

Facts

Meredith Boucher was an assistant store manager at a Wal-Mart in Ontario, Canada (Boucher v Wal-Mart Canada Corp., 2014). Jason Pinnock, her manager, requested her to falsify a store temperature log. She refused.

Details surrounding the case appear to show Pinnock subsequently began a campaign of:

- berating

- humiliating
- profane language
- taunting
- criticizing
- disciplinary action

Prior to quitting, Boucher attempted to address her concerns with management through the open-door policy. Although the policy stated anything discussed was to remain confidential, Pinnock heard about it.

Despite sufficient evidence and employee witnesses to back Boucher's complaints, Wal-Mart concluded Boucher's complaints were unfounded and that she was trying to undermine Pinnock's authority.

Regardless of Pinnock recognizing the effects (weight loss, poor appetite, insomnia, ill health) of his behaviour toward Boucher, he indicated his intention was to continue until she quit.

Boucher finally quit and sued.

Issues

Did Pinnock's treatment of Boucher constitute constructive dismissal? Was she eligible for aggravated and punitive damages?

Decision

Meredith Boucher was found to be constructively dismissed. She was originally awarded 20 weeks' severance, $1,000,000 in punitive damages, $200,000 in aggravated damages against Wal-Mart, plus $100,000 for intentional infliction of suffering and $150,000 in punitive damages against Pinnock, for which Wal-Mart was vicariously responsible.

This was appealed. As a result, the punitive damages of $1,000,000 were reduced to $100,000, but the $200,000 for aggravated was upheld. The $100,000 of intentional infliction of suffering by Pinnock was upheld, while the $150,000 in punitive was reduced to $10,000.

Rationale

Meredith Boucher was constructively dismissed. Wal-Mart (and Pinnock) acted in bad faith with their treatment towards Boucher, along with their failure to be fair and honest.

Additionally, Wal-Mart failed to conduct a fair investigation, and was negligent in addressing the poor conduct of Pinnock. As a result, Wal-Mart was vicariously responsible for his conduct.

Wallace v United Grain Growers Ltd., 1997 332 (SCC), [1997] 3 SCR 701

Facts

Jack Wallace was recruited by the United Grain Growers' printing and publishing division (Wallace v United Grain Growers Ltd., 1997).

During the recruitment, he expressed his concern about moving to another company at the age of 45. He was given assurances that he would continue working for United Grain Growers until his retirement, providing he performed as expected. Jack was the top salesperson every year of his employment with UGG.

Despite this, he was terminated in 1986, in the presence of his co-workers, and without explanation.

Jack Wallace filed a statement of claim citing wrongful dismissal. United Grain Growers cited in their statement of defence that Wallace had been dismissed with cause. Accusations were then made against Wallace. As a result, his future job prospects were damaged.

Issues

Was Jack Wallace wrongfully dismissed? Were United Grain Growers' actions toward Wallace enough to warrant aggravated damages? Can action be brought forth for bad-faith discharge?

Decision

Wallace was awarded a 24-month notice period at trial. In addition to that, he was award $15,000 in aggravated damages for mental distress due to United Grain Growers' conduct.

This was appealed, and the 24 months was reduced to 15 months, and the award of $15,000 for aggravated damages was overturned.

The case went on to the Supreme Court, where it was noted that employers owed employees the duty of good faith and fair dealing in the matter of dismissal. Should this be violated, the employee may be eligible for additional compensation for aggravated damages. This later became known as "Wallace damages."

Following is an excerpt from the Wallace v United Grain Growers case itself:

> However, where an employee can establish that an employer engaged in bad faith conduct or unfair dealing in the course of dismissal, injuries such as humiliation, embarrassment and damage to one's sense of self-worth and self-esteem might all be worthy of compensation depending upon the circumstances of the case. In these situations, compensation does not flow from the fact of dismissal itself, but rather from the manner in which the dismissal was effected by the employer. *(Supreme Court of Canada, 1997)*

Rationale

The manner of dismissal is now a significant factor upon determining a reasonable notice period.

As a result of this case, several key areas were identified that may lead to Wallace damages:

1. Making false accusations

2. Damaging the employee's prospects of finding another job

3. Misrepresenting the reasons for termination

4. Firing the employee to ensure deprivation of a benefit

5. Firing the employee in front of co-workers (Wallace v United Grain Growers Ltd, 2021)

Pilon v Peugeot Canada Ltd. (1980) was one of many cited. Pilon was the first successful case of mental distress damages in employment law.

Also cited was *Vorvis v Insurance Corporation of British Columbia* (1989), as it pertained to Wallace and damages for mental distress, loss of reputation and prestige, and punitive damages.

Honda Canada Inc. v Keays, 2008 SCC 39 (CanLII), [2008] 2 SCR 362

Facts

Keays was initially hired to work on an assembly line for Honda (Honda Canada Inc. v Keays, 2008). During his 11-year employment, he moved to a position in data entry.

He was diagnosed with chronic fatigue syndrome (CFS) in 1997. He was off work on disability insurance until 1998, when the insurance company decided he could return full time.

The Honda company's disability program (often better known as a return-to-work program) allowed for Keays to miss work as long as a valid doctor's note was provided.

Keays absences persisted and increased. According to Honda, the doctor's notes were becoming increasingly cryptic. Therefore, Honda requested Keays meet with a specialist appointed by Honda.

As a result, Keays retained counsel and requested further clarification as to the purpose of the assessment.

A power struggled ensued, which eventually ended with Keays' termination.

Keays sued for wrongful dismissal.

Issues

Was Keays wrongfully dismissed? Was Keays discriminated against? Was there harassment/misconduct against Keays? Are punitive and/or aggravated damages applicable?

Decision

The determination of wrongful dismissal, along with Honda also committing acts of discrimination, harassment, and misconduct were determined. Keays was awarded 15 months' pay for wrongful dismissal. As well, Keays was awarded punitive damages of $500,000 and an increase of the notice period to 24 months.

The Supreme Court of Justice upheld the wrongful dismissal; however, it removed the other damages. As a result, the award was reduced to 15 months' notice.

Rationale

Keays was wrongfully dismissed. The reasonable notice period was determined to be 15 months. With the "Wallace Bump" (*Wallace v United Grain Growers*), this was increased by another nine months due to Honda's bad-faith dealings in his termination and resulting medical consequences. As well, Honda was ordered to pay $500,000 in punitive damages.

This was appealed. While the 15 months reasonable notice remained, the punitive damages were reduced to $100,000.

The Supreme Court judge agreed Keays had been harassed and discriminated against, as well as retaliated against.

The *Wallace v United Grain Growers* case was significant for *Keays v Honda*. Both were determined to be cases of wrongful dismissal. *Bardal v Globe and Mail* was another influential case (1960).

BC Public Service Employee Relations Commission v BCGSEU, 1999 652 (SCC), [1999] 3 SCR 3

Facts

Tawney Meiorin was a firefighter in BC. She had performed her duties satisfactorily for three years when a new physical assessment test was implemented (British Columbia [Public Service Employee Relations Commission] v BCGSEU, 1999). Despite taking the test four times, she was unsuccessful. As a result, she was dismissed from her position.

A grievance was filed by her union, citing discrimination on the basis of sex. Both Meiorin and the union claimed that the aerobic testing resulted in a form of constructive discrimination. This was due to it having an adverse result for females. It was suggested by the union that the aerobic standards for women be lowered.

Issues

Does the new physical assessment test constitute adverse discrimination?

Decision

Originally awarded reinstatement by an arbitrator, this case was then appealed by the province of BC. The BC Court of Appeals then ruled in favour of BC. The final appeal, to the Supreme Court of Canada, is where the new test for reasonable accommodation (also known as the "Meiorin Test") was developed.

With this test, an employer can justify the impugned standard by establishing on the balance of probabilities:

1. that the employer adopted the standard for a purpose rationally connected to the performance of the job

2. that the employer adopted the particular standard in an honest and good faith belief that it was necessary to the fulfillment of that legitimate work-related purpose

3. that the standard was reasonably necessary to the accomplishment of that legitimate work-related purpose. To show that the standard is reasonably necessary, it must be demonstrated that it is impossible to accommodate individual employees sharing the characteristics of the claimant without imposing undue hardship upon the employer (British Columbia [Public Service Employee Relations Commission] v British Columbia Government Service Employees' Union, 2019).

Rationale

Workplace policies and standards need to be designed so that they do not discriminate.

The Meiorin test above is now utilized to determine if workplace standards can be justified.

Lalonde v Sena Solid Waste Holdings Inc., 2017 ABQB 374

Facts

After four years of working for Sena Solid Waste and what seemed like any other workday, Lalonde was called to a meeting with the maintenance manager (Lalonde v Sena Solid Waste Holdings Inc., 2017).

At the meeting, Lalonde was accused of insubordination and putting a co-worker's life in danger. According to the maintenance manager, Lalonde was supposed to supervise the co-worker. The insubordination referred to what appeared to be a misunderstanding regarding some scrap metal.

Lalonde attempted to clarify the allegations against him. He tried to explain that he was not advised that he was responsible for his co-worker. However, he was not provided the opportunity to do so, or to clarify the details regarding the scrap metal. Lalonde was suspended and escorted off the property by two employees.

During his suspension, Lalonde attempted to contact the maintenance manager by telephoning and writing to him.

He heard nothing for several weeks, which added to his stress level. Lalonde ended up off on stress leave. His sick notes covered the time from July 3, 2012, to July 30, 2012.

On July 24, 2012, Lalonde received a letter of termination, stating:

> This letter confirms your employment with SENA Waste Services will end effective July 24, 2012. After which you will no longer be considered an active employee. You're being terminated with cause due to your failure to follow safety procedures and your failure to follow your supervisor's instructions. (Lalonde v Sena Solid Waste Holdings Inc., 2017)

Lalonde wrote to the division manager two days later as a last resort. In the letter, he provided detailed responses to the allegations, along with questions of his own.

Lalonde received an email in August from the human resource manager. That email was copied to other senior managers, identifying what claimed to be failures of Lalonde's regarding safety.

As a response, Lalonde filed a statement of claim for wrongful dismissal.

Sena Solid Waste, in turn, filed a statement of defence. It detailed the alleged reasons for dismissal. However, upon opening day of the 2017 trial, Sena withdrew their allegation for cause.

Facts were clarified during the trial. One of these facts included a letter from another co-worker present at the tailgate meeting. The letter confirmed Lalonde's assertion that he was not aware of or advised he was responsible for the co-worker who had not obtained a permit.

A letter written by Lalonde's wife was included within the trial as evidence. The letter noted the impacts of the dismissal, the humiliation from being escorted off the property, as well as the treatment from Sena management and human resources. Lalonde continued to have mental health problems, which included being depressed, miserable, isolated, and angry.

Issues

Do the employment letters signed by Lalonde limit the amount of notice to which he is entitled? What is the reasonable/appropriate notice period? Is Lalonde entitled to punitive damages? Was the investigation properly conducted?

Decision

It was determined that Lalonde was wrongfully dismissed without just cause. He was awarded six months as a notice period and awarded $75,000 for aggravated damages.

There are numerous summaries written by lawyers, as well as news articles. The CanLII analysis indicates, in part, that "the investigation was at best incompetent and unfair and at worst a sham" (Lalonde v Sena Solid Waste Holdings Inc., 2017).

Wallace v United Grain Growers is referred to with regards to discussion on determining reasonable/appropriate notice. Also included in this discussion is the case of *Bardal v Globe & Mail Ltd.* Besides the Wallace case, the Bardal case makes note of the following factors:

1. The nature of the employment – the more senior the position, the longer it is likely to take to find a replacement position. There are fewer senior management jobs around.

2. The length of service – the longer an employee has worked for one employer, the more difficult it may be to find an alternate job, either because the employee has narrowed his or her skills by working for one employer for a long time, or the employee has been paid more than the job is worth because of long service.

3. The age of the employee – the older the employee is, the less likely he or she is to find a suitable position, or the longer it is likely to take. Older employees are sometimes perceived as less worthwhile to invest in.

4. The availability of suitable similar employment in regard to the employee's experience, training, and qualifications together with

surrounding economic circumstances – what is the realistic prospect of this employee getting a similar replacement job? What is the job market like? In good economic times, jobs may be plentiful and the employee may have little difficulty finding a good replacement job; in poorer times, there may be few jobs around (Lalonde v Sena Solid Waste Holdings Inc., 2017).

As well, while the company claims to have undertaken an investigation, Lalonde's input was never requested. Also noted in the CanLII, "The evidence supports the conclusion that the internal investigation was essentially a sham" (Lalonde v Sena Solid Waste Holdings Inc., 2017).

Other case law, such as *Boucher v Wal-Mart* and *Karmel v Calgary Jewish Academy (2015)*, was referenced pertaining to aggravated damages. False reasons for dismissal, abusive conduct leading up to dismissal, and unfair investigation all showed a lack of procedural fairness and thus reason for aggravated damages. After consideration, Lalonde was awarded $75,000 for aggravated damages.

The equivalent of six months' salary, with allowance for both short-term and long-term retention bonuses, was allowed for reasonable notice. Money earned during the six months was deducted from the amount.

Punitive damages were dismissed.

Rationale

Treatment from Sena to Lalonde prior to and after termination was reprehensible. As with Boucher, they failed in their duty of good faith as an employer.

The reasonable notice period provided was insufficient. In determining an appropriate notice period, the Bardal case (as noted) provided clearer insight.

Perez-Moreno v Kulczycki, 2013 HRTO 1074 (CanLII)

Facts

Perez-Moreno, a manager at a golf and country club, intervened in an argument between Kulczycki and another co-worker (Perez-Moreno v Kulczyski, 2013).

Kulczycki later made comments that Perez-Moreno testified as being "humiliating and damaging to his character, work and personal life" and "created a negative emotional, social, mental, and possibly financial effect on him" (Minkin, 2013). One of the posts noted she had been written up for calling her manager "a dirty Mexican" (Perez-Moreno v Kulczyski, 2013).

Added to this was the negative impact on Perez-Moreno's son. A classmate informed him of the posts the following day in school, who Perez-Moreno said "should not have to feel ashamed of his roots" (Perez-Moreno v Kulczyski, 2013).

Issues

Do comments made on Facebook regarding a supervisor amount to harassment under the *Ontario Human Rights Code*?

Decision

Kulczycki knew or ought to have known that her comments would have been unwelcomed by Perez-Moreno.

Perez-Moreno did not name his employer, even though he could have. Instead, he requested to have Kulczycki removed from the workplace.

The Tribunal does not have the authority to remove Kulczycki from the workplace. Instead, they ordered her to complete the Ontario Human Rights Commission's online training, "Human Rights 101."

Rationale

The analysis of this case states,

> Subsection 5(2) of the *Code* prohibits harassment in the workplace on the basis of race, origin, ancestry and citizenship. Section 10(1) defines harassment as "a course of vexatious comment or conduct that is known or ought reasonably to be known to be unwelcome." (Perez-Moreno v Kulczyski, 2013)

Elgert v Home Hardware Stores Limited, 2011 ABCA 112

Facts

Daniel John Elgert was a supervisor at Home Hardware. He was employed with Home Hardware for 17 years. One problematic employee was Christa Bernier. Christa's father was Elgert's boss.

Due to Christa's ongoing problematic behaviour, Elgert had her transferred to another area. After being transferred to another area, Christa Bernier made a claim to her father that Elgert had sexually harassed her (Elgert v Home Hardware Stores Limited, 2011).

What transpired afterwards was a shoddy investigation, as noted in the case itself. The investigator had little to no training or experience in investigations. This investigator was also a long-time friend of Norris Bernier, the father of Christa Bernier.

Elgert was terminated "for cause," with the letter citing sexual harassment and insubordination as grounds for his dismissal. When he had asked the investigator what he was accused of, he was told, "You know what you did" (Elgert v Home Hardware Stores Limited, 2011). Elgert was never interviewed or provided the opportunity to provide his defence. He was escorted from the building and was not allowed to return for his belongings. Prior to the investigation, Elgert's son (who also worked at

Home Hardware) was advised by the investigator of his father's suspension for sexual harassment. This investigator indicated his father would not have been suspended if he wasn't 100 per cent certain of his guilt. A petition with names and numbers of co-workers supporting Elgert was circulated; however, none of them were interviewed.

Elgert sued for wrongful dismissal and defamation.

Issues

Was Daniel Elgert wrongfully dismissed? Is he eligible for aggravated damages? Are punitive damages warranted? What are the implications of the poorly conducted interview?

Decision

The Alberta Court of Queen's Bench trial determined that Elgert did not commit the sexual assault. And conduct by Home Hardware was in bad faith, as well as "harsh, vindictive, reprehensible, malicious, and extreme in nature" (Elgert v Home Hardware Stores Limited, 2011). Elgert was awarded 24 months of pay in lieu of notice, $60,000 for defamation, $200,000 for aggravated damages, and $300,000 for punitive damages.

As with many cases, the decision was appealed. As a result, the $200,000 was removed, as it was indicated that Elgert had not provided evidence of mental distress. And the punitive damages were found to be inordinately high. The punitive damages were then lowered to $75,000.

Rationale

Honda v Keays and *Wallace v United Grain Growers* were both cited as examples, as they are also excellent cases of wrongful dismissal and aggravated damages.

Elgert, like those in the above examples, dealt with harsh, vindictive, and malicious conduct from an employer.

In addition to the reprehensible behaviour from the employer, the investigation was poorly conducted. Important points for any business to consider from this case include the significance of fair, timely, and unbiased investigations.

As with the other noted cases, *Elgert v Home Hardware* is being used as case law for other cases, particularly regarding investigations in the workplace (Elgert v Home Hardware Stores Limited, 2011).

Greenwood v Canada, 2020 FC 119 (CanLII)

Facts

The RCMP was labelled as having a culture of dysfunction in the 2017 report on workplace harassment. The class action filed cites a toxic work environment, which includes workplace harassment and bullying (Greenwood v Canada, 2020).

Geoffrey Greenwood and Todd Gray were spearheading the class action.

Within the RCMP was a culture of bullying, intimidation, and harassment that went on for decades (Gerster, 2020).

Both Greenwood and Gray advised of their experiences, along with responses and retaliation suffered as a result. Systemic bullying, physical and psychological injuries, financial losses, and career limitations were all noted. Some of the evidence cited were various reports on harassment within the RCMP. These reports were over the course of ten years and indicate the inability of the current internal processes to address the toxic culture within.

Affidavits from several high-level directors within the RCMP and Veterans Affairs were included by the Crown. The Crown also included supporting documents against proceeding with a class action. The Crown indicated the internal processes and legislative remedies available to them, and they note the core issues are workplace disputes, which are more appropriately dealt with internally.

The class action includes members and civilian members of the RCMP.

Issues

Noted within the certified class action case are questions regarding negligence and damages. These questions are as follows:

Negligence

1. Did the RCMP, through its agents, servants and employees owe a duty of care to the plaintiffs and other Primary Class Members to take reasonable steps in the operation or management of the Force to provide them with a work environment free from bullying, intimidation and harassment?

2. If yes, was there a breach of this duty by the RCMP through its agents, servants and employees?

3. If yes, was the Crown vicariously liable for the failure of its agents, servants and employees at the RCMP, to take reasonable steps in the operation and management of the Force to provide a work environment free from bullying, intimidation and harassment?

Damages

4. Can the Court make an aggregate assessment of any damages as part of the common issues trial? If so, to whom? In what amount?

5. Does the conduct justify an award of aggravated, exemplary and/or punitive damages? (Greenwood v Canada, 2020)

Decision

ORDER in T-1201-18 certified it as a class action.

Greenwood and Gray were listed as representative plaintiffs. Those eligible included a wide breadth of people:

> All persons who reside in Canada who were or are Regular Members, Special Constables Members, Reservists, Supernumerary Special Constables, Civilian Members, and Public Service Employees under s. 10 of

the *Royal Canadian Mounted Police Act*, RSC 1985, c R-10, Volunteers, Auxiliary Constables, Non-Profit Employees, Temporary Civilian Employees, Casual Employees, Term Employees, Cadets, Pre-Cadets, Students, Contract Employees, Municipal Employees, and others who work or worked with the RCMP (the "Class"); and

All individuals who are entitled to assert a claim pursuant to the *Family Law Act*, RSO 1990 c F.3, and equivalent or comparable legislation in other provinces and territories (the "Family Class"). (Greenwood v Canada, 2020)

Rationale

Griffin v Dell Canada Inc is cited as a partial reasoning as to why and how the class action could proceed (2009).

As noted in a Global News article, Justice Ann Marie McDonald stated, "I am not satisfied that the claims could be fully adjudicated through the available internal mechanisms" (Gerster, 2020).

Other Canadian Cases of Interest

This section documents recent cases of interest. While these cases are (of yet) not part of Canadian case law, they are recent examples of bullying and harassment that have made the news.

Robert Duhaime and the RM of Parkdale

This case involves suicide attributed to the workplace.

Robert Duhaime was a grader operator for the RM of Parkdale in Saskatchewan. His death by suicide (August 31, 2017) was attributed to his workplace (Bridges, The doc project: Her husband took his own life after he was bullied on the job, 2018a).

While Duhaime's widow noted that the weather was the causative factor for the condition of the roads, he suffered as a result. As a grader operator, Duhaime received telephone calls from councillors and staff regarding their dissatisfaction over the roads he graded. And there were situations wherein he was belittled in front of colleagues.

A letter from WCB to the RM (a copy of which was also provided to his widow) states that Robert "experienced interpersonal incidents that were excessive and unusual in comparison to pressures and tensions experienced in normal employment" (Bridges, 2018b).

Robert Duhaime had been dealing with mental health issues unrelated to the workplace for approximately 18 years. However, on his doctor's advice, he went off on stress leave in 2018 due to his ongoing workplace problems.

In a formal complaint, Duhaime named his alleged abusers. On the second day back to work from his stress leave, one of the persons named in the complaint confronted Duhaime. The following day, Robert Duhaime was found unresponsive. He had committed suicide.

The Workers' Compensation Board (WCB) ruled in favour of recognizing that Duhaime's suicide was a result of his workplace.

While the rural municipality filed an appeal, the decision was upheld. Duhaime's widow was provided an initial payment to cover expenses, including her husband's funeral. Workers' Compensation also offered her monthly compensation for five years following his death.

Mrs. Duhaime continued to fight for accountability. Besides speaking to the media, she wrote to both the premier at the time, Scott Moe, and the justice minister.

Further details can be found through CBC Radio's *The doc project*, which has documented Duhaime's fight for justice (Bridges, The doc project: Her husband took his own life after he was bullied on the job, 2018a; The doc project: The grader operator's widow, 2018).

CUPE Local 500 and City of Winnipeg

CUPE, a union representing some of the employees in the City of Winnipeg, sent a letter outlining concerns to the mayor and council. This letter alleged inaction over employee's complaints of racism, bullying, and harassment.

A CTV news article titled "Union alleges 'toxic workplace' for City of Winnipeg employees facing racism, bullying and harassment" (Unger, 2020) notes a number of concerns. For one, it indicates that it took months for initial investigation meetings to take place. Employees raising concerns continue to be victimized, as reported in September 2020 by CTV News (Unger).

In February 2021, another article was featured by the Winnipeg Sun (Snell, 2021). It calls out the Winnipeg mayor with regards to the previous letter sent regarding racism, bullying, and harassment.

The letter again notes the City's inability and lack of willingness to address the above concerns. As a result, employees who raise concerns continue to be victimized, culminating in a toxic environment (Snell, 2021).

Calgary Police Service

Jen Magnus publicly resigned at a Calgary Police Commission meeting in 2017 (Bell, 2017). Assertions included bullying, sexual harassment, and degradation. She had worked with the Calgary Police Service for 14 years.

Jen, as well as 12 other members within the Calgary Police Service, filed bullying and harassment complaints.

It takes great courage for anyone to speak out about bullying and/or harassment situations, as those dealing with such situations will undoubtedly agree.

And yet, from appearances, Jen Magnus and numerous others dealt with the ongoing and systematic bullying for a number of years.

Perhaps, as many of us who are being or have been bullied can relate, a career means more to many than just a job. It may have been a passion and/or a calling to some.

Many of us work diligently toward careers. As such, we don't want to give up that for which we've worked hard and sacrificed. This could be time away from family, for one, or time and energy on coursework and other forms of education toward what may have been a dream job.

When someone or something gets in the way of that dream, many will attempt to work through their difficulties in hopes of preserving their passion. And, when forces beyond their control dictate choices, most are unprepared and often resist having to leave what they have worked and given up so much for. The end result can be devastating.

I sympathize and completely agree with Jen, who states, "I believe every employee in Canada has a right to a safe and respectful workplace and the Calgary police should be no different" (Bell, 2017).

Concerning is an internal workplace review of the Calgary Police Service (CPS), which was conducted in 2013 (Bell, 2017). This review included allegations of sexual assault, sexual harassment, bullying, intimidation, and retaliation.

There are numerous concerns as to why these serious allegations were continuing to be a problem. Even more troublesome, this was occurring within an organization that is supposed to uphold the law.

If we cannot trust law enforcement to treat one another with respect and dignity, there is a problem. Everyone within any branch of law enforcement (male and female) should treat each other with respect. And, if they do not, it needs to be addressed.

When the public sees this happen on an ongoing basis, for years, their respect is lost. As most of us are aware, once trust or respect is lost, it takes a long time to earn it back.

City of Edmonton

Numerous articles indicate a wealth of information regarding the City of Edmonton's toxic culture. The details include examples of workplace bullying, harassment, discrimination, retaliation, and poor management.

According to a number of different survey results, the percentages of employees feeling they were harassed were:

- 2014 17.6% (Heidenreich, 2019)
- 2016 19% (Heidenreich, 2019)
- 2017 20% (Simons, 2017)
- 2018 23.8% (Heidenreich, 2019)

Despite the surveys, media coverage, vigils, and probes, the toxic culture appears to persist.

The November 2018 article "Vigil highlights harassment, bullying at City of Edmonton" cites 235 complaints from January to November of that year. A corporate audit showed that nearly 20% of staff who responded to a survey feel they have been harassed.

Another article the following January reports the 2018 survey to have an additional increase of 4% to almost 24% of those being harassed in the City of Edmonton (Vigil highlights harassment, bullying at City of Edmonton, 2018).

While a safe disclosure office was opened in 2019, another newer article notes that only 39% of employees were aware of it (Cook, "This is clearly problematic": Most City of Edmonton employees not speaking up about discrimination or inappropriate behaviour, workplace survey highlights, 2020b). With the ongoing and increasing percentages of harassment/bullying within the workplace, it is troublesome that most were unaware of this.

The newest survey completed in 2020 provided that only 51% feel they can speak their minds without consequences and only 52% have confidence in the executive leadership team (Cook, 2020a).

This article by the Edmonton Journal also noted several city employees had contacted them to advise they have been bullied or harassed

(Cook D. , October 22, 2020). However, they were not willing to go on record. Here is a link to the article:

https://edmontonjournal.com/news/local-news/city-of-edmonton-workforce-survey-results

It has been several years since the first survey noted in 2014. To paraphrase other sources, particularly regarding sexual harassment, time's up. Whether it is the City of Edmonton or any other city (or organization, for that matter), all employees deserve better. Everyone deserves a respectful workplace, free from harassment and bullying.

International Cases of Note

Many, if not all, of the noted cases were Canadian. As most of us are aware, workplace bullying and harassment is a worldwide phenomenon.

There are a vast number of cases worldwide that are equally deserving of attention. The following are just a few.

France Telecom (now Orange) Restructuring Harassment

Didier Lombard was CEO of a telecom company in France. He was reported as having indicated he would get rid of employees one way or another, whether through the window or the door.

With a reported $55 million debt, executives were noted as attempting to rid the company of in excess of 20,000 employees as part of a restructuring plan (Nossiter, 2019).

Management allegedly conducted a campaign of harassment to encourage resignations. In this conscious scheme, employees were forced into unsuitable positions, resulting in a toxic environment.

While this campaign worked, it caused enough distress for 35 workers to die by suicide and numerous other attempted suicides. It became noted as "institutional moral harassment" (Nossiter, 2019).

Methods of suicide were various. One set himself on fire in a parking lot of one of the telecom's locations. Another one jumped off a bridge on a highway in the Alps. And a woman leapt from a sixth story office window. Many cases included suicide notes pointing to the workplace as the cause.

Charged included:

- The company itself, charged the maximum penalty of $83,000.
- Dieder Lombard, the former chief executive of France Telecom. He was sentenced to four months in prison and fined $16,000.
- Second in command, Louis-Pierre Wenès, sentenced to four months imprisonment and a $16,000 fine.
- Former human resources director, Olivier Barberot, was also charged $16,000 and received a sentence of four months in prison.

The three men noted above were found guilty of creating a working environment "full of fear that led directly to the suicides and other attempted suicides of several employees" (Ormondi, 2019).

Toyota Work-Related Suicide

Toyota was found responsible for the suicide of an employee by a Japanese Labour official.

An employee committed suicide inside Toyota's dormitory. Workplace bullying was cited as contributing to his suicide.

The 28-year-old engineer was regularly ridiculed about his background in education, constantly insulted, and repeatedly called an idiot by his boss.

Further details can be found in a number of articles, including the *Globe & Mail*, which indicates that the "case came amid growing awareness of problems with what the Japanese call 'power harassment'" (Kageyama, 2019).

Poor leadership breeds toxic workplace cultures. Allowing poor leadership to perpetuate further imbeds the toxicity within the workplace. The preceding examples show poor leadership, along with poor behaviour.

CHAPTER 13:
Case Study – My Experience with the Peter Principle

So, here I was, working in an organization that was theoretically bureaucratic. There were some employees in leadership positions who were clear examples of the Peter principle. These underqualified and often insecure people were the ones in leadership positions, and often referred to staff as ownership (my girls, my staff, etc.). And should you even hint at questioning someone's authority (even the co-worker with a few years experience), you were quickly reminded as to who they were in relation to you.

In my story in chapter 7, there are a number of points that reflect the poor leadership of my supervisor, as well as others within. One example is when I attempted to address my concerns, only to have her hold her hand up to silence me and refuse to speak to me. Or, when my co-worker was caught in the act of framing me for her mistakes, she simply looked over and shrugged her shoulders. And the numerous incidents where she simply went with what the co-worker would tell her I may or may not have done, even after this co-worker was caught trying to frame me for her mistakes. This supervisor would restrict time away, including funerals as a result of my co-worker's complaints. Records of discussions were added to at the suggestions of this co-worker, with no questions directed at me. The supervisor would also join this co-worker in telling me not to assist someone over the telephone with the new payroll program. A good supervisor would realize that internal customers are important, as is providing assistance with educating and coaching others in order to help us reduce errors and get payroll done on time. Those are just a few notable examples of this supervisor as it relates to the Peter principle.

Regardless, she was talented and very knowledgeable as it pertains to payroll. She understood the intricacies of payroll well. She did a phenomenal job of setting up the new payroll program as a result. Because of her knowledge, she was promoted within to the supervisor position. However, she simply did not have the skills necessary for someone in a supervisory position.

As a supervisor, one needs to understand both the jobs of those they affect, but also the variety of duties as a supervisor.

When and if someone in a leadership position is lacking essential skills, either they or the person(s) they report to should recognize and ensure they are addressed.

If the lacking essential skills can be addressed with further education and/or training, it is necessary to do so. Unfortunately, all too often, this is missed. And, as a result, the given employee remains in a position in which they are incompetent.

CHAPTER 14:
Progressive Discipline

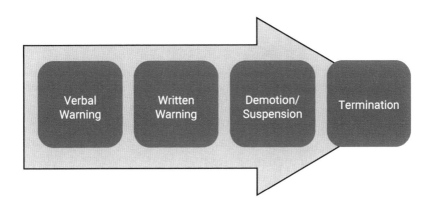

Figure 14.3 The progressive discipline model.

While the illustration in Fig. 14.3 is theoretically correct, there is more to progressive discipline than some realize.

This could be an opportunity for improvement for both sides. Perhaps there needs to be better communication of expectations from leadership. Or more training may be needed. Is information lacking? Is there something going on in an employee's life that is impacting their work? Is the employee overloaded? Is it possible (as in my situation) they have been set up, framed by another co-worker? Could there be a toxic environment? Could some time off alleviate the stress? In certain situations (e.g., family stresses, workplace harassment/bullying), would counselling services help? Ongoing dialogue and increased understanding and awareness on both sides of progressive discipline can be of assistance for employee *and* employer.

For an employee, there are a number of reasons that progressive discipline may assist them. When used appropriately, the employee may better understand the expectations that are required of them. The expectations are (or should be) clearly laid out. Ongoing discussions on what is being done properly, what needs to be done, and how employer and employee can work together to achieve this should occur. If an employee has any concerns or questions, these can be addressed with them. This can be a useful tool if both parties are willing to work toward a common goal.

For those within unionized environments, the employee is normally contacted ahead of time. They are (or should be) advised of their right to bring a union representative. Having a union representative provides an employee with someone who should know their contract and their rights. As well, it is often helpful to have another person in attendance to hear and simply understand the process, offering them support and guidance.

It is extremely important to note that progressive discipline is not meant to be utilized as a tool to "encourage" an employee to leave; however, there are employers who choose to use it in this manner.

Toxic or poor leadership sometimes attempts to utilize progressive discipline to get rid of employees for a number of reasons. As this book deals primarily with bullying and harassment, the following example is the first to come to mind.

Poor leadership will attempt to find ways to avoid properly dealing with uncomfortable situations. They may initially attempt to ignore the problem, hoping it will go away. Or leadership may view employees with ongoing problems as whiners and problematic employees, and may characterize the employee's behaviour as childish or requiring "babysitting." Leaders who do this may miss signs of workplace harassment or bullying, such as DARVO or scapegoating.

As a result of their perceptions of the employee's behaviour, the person in the leadership position decides to utilize this tool improperly. The case study in chapter 7 is an example of this.

Typical Steps of Progressive Discipline

*Note: As an effective leader, compassion can go a long way in every step.

1. Verbal Warning

The manager or supervisor meets with the employee. Normally, the employee is contacted ahead of time and a mutually agreed time and place are advised. If the employee is unionized, they should be advised of their ability to bring a union representative.

The issues and concerns at hand are verbally discussed. In some organizations, there may be something called a record of discussion (ROD). But this is *not* written up until *after* the discussion.

If what led to the verbal warning is the result of a simple misunderstanding, this process ends at the first step. However, if there is a timeline, training, and/or expectations on improvements, the employee is advised of these.

2. Written Warning

If, after the verbal warning, the *same* problem(s) persists, then the employee is contacted again, and another meeting is scheduled. As with step one, if the person is unionized, they are advised of their right to bring a union representative.

As this is normally a stressful and embarrassing time for the given employee, consideration on the timing and location of the meeting is important. But this should be of consideration on each step.

The written warning includes details of the verbal warning. Performance issues, particularly unresolved ones noted in the verbal step are noted once again. The expectations of the employee are included, along with what will happen should expectations not be met: termination, PIP, or demotion.

This is where some in leadership positions fail and simply hand an employee the written discipline, which may include additional problems noted on the written discipline.

3. Demotion or Suspension or Performance Improvement Plan

If there continues to be no improvement (on the same issue[s]), this is when an employee might be demoted back to a previous position, placed in a less demanding position, suspended, or put on a performance improvement plan (PIP).

A PIP specifically outlines objectives and expectations, and timelines in which these are expected to be met. Expectations are determined in a meeting and then written out in a PIP. This is clearly laid out for all parties (employee, supervisor, union representative) to understand.

4. Termination

If, after all of the above steps have been properly utilized, there has been little to no improvement, an employee may then be terminated.

This should be a last resort. In many cases, both parties normally want to avoid getting to this point.

There continues to be some misconception(s) as to the proper application of progressive discipline and the process(es) involved in it. This could be for a variety of reasons, including:

- Inexperienced, untrained staff (whether it be supervisor, manager, director, or HR)
- Lack of knowledge or training of the person in the leadership position
- Improper application of progressive discipline
- Toxic work culture
- Use of progressive discipline as a tool to dismiss employees

Utilized *properly*, performance management can be effective for both employers and employees. Properly utilizing a progressive disciplinary plan can lead to numerous benefits, such as:

1. Assists both employees and their leaders in recognizing areas where improvement is needed
2. Provides supervisors/management the ability to recognize and address problematic behaviour sooner rather than later
3. Increases the chances of better communication between management and staff
4. Supports employees and employers toward higher productivity
5. Provides employees a clearer understanding as to why/how they are being disciplined
6. May expose issues, such as workplace bullying, requiring attention/action by leadership
7. Handled properly, it encourages consistency and fairness for all

While each organization's progressive discipline plan may vary slightly, the following is a more thorough discussion of progressive discipline's general steps and guidelines.

Step 1: Verbal Warning

(This can be done one or more times)
A verbal warning may seem self-explanatory. However, the following should be completed at the time of the verbal warning:

- Advise the employee if the verbal warning is part of progressive discipline
- Offer and/or provide any coaching/training needed by the employee
- Advise the employee of the timeline being provided before moving to the next step in progressive discipline

This discussion (verbal warning) may provide a better insight into a variety of things, such as:

- need for additional training

- misunderstandings
- toxicity
    - e.g., a co-worker providing false information regarding policies/procedures
    - ongoing bullying/harassment
    - gaslighting via another employee (supervisor/manager/co-worker)
    - DARVO
- personal/professional insight. For example, an employee may be under undue stress (e.g., terminally ill family member)

Items included within the verbal discussion may include:

- concerns or issues the supervisor has regarding the employee and their performance
- additional training, if needed
- discussion of policies involved, along with providing copies of applicable policies (e.g., advising if the discussion is a part of progressive discipline)

Once there is actually a *private and verbal* discussion between the supervisor and employee, it can be documented.

Note: Please, please, please discuss this with the given employee *before* documenting. It is impossible to know all of the given particulars/facts prior to having a discussion. It is shocking to see people in such positions doing just the opposite.

Example: Jane is habitually late coming to work. The supervisor (or a designate, such as an assistant) contacts Jane and requests her to meet with the supervisor. A date and time are determined and, if unionized, she is given the ability to bring a union representative.

At the meeting, Jane is advised of her tardiness. Examples of dates and times are advised. She is also told that the meeting is part of a progressive discipline plan. If she continues to be late for work, it will result in a written warning and the consequences/next steps will be laid out in the progressive discipline plan.

Step 2: Written Warning

(This can occur one or more times before moving to the next step.)
The written warning is a formal letter from the person in the leadership position to the employee. It outlines the issue(s) at hand. It notes the steps taken to date, ongoing expectations, and further action that may occur if improvement is not made.

- Advise the employee again if it is part of progressive discipline
- Again, advise the employee of any coaching or advice needed
- Advise on the timeline being provided before moving to the next step in progressive discipline

Despite the verbal warning, the *same issue/concern* from step one to this point has not been resolved. Note that step two is *not* to be used for a *different* issue or concern from the verbal warning.

For example, Jane was advised of her late arrivals being unsatisfactory and told that further occurrences would result in a written warning. As her lateness has continued, a written warning was issued. Often, reference to the specific policy is made, along with what further occurrences may result in (e.g., suspension/demotion, PIP, or possibility of termination).

Ensure the employee is provided the opportunity to respond to the concerns discussed and provide their input.

Step 3: Suspension, Demotion, or PIP

Step 3 is the suspension or demotion of an employee, or the implementation of a PIP. Each situation is unique. Often, in situations where an employee continues with undesirable behaviour (e.g., Jane), a suspension of hours or days may occur. Normally, most employees realize the seriousness and the behaviour is modified.

Another option is a demotion. Sometimes it is a demotion to a previous position where the given employee was performing satisfactorily.

Or, other times, it may be to another position within the organization in what is considered a lower position.

The final option is a PIP (Performance Improvement Plan) may be implemented. With this, there is a plan with the improvements laid out. Sometimes, this may involve further training. Deficiencies that need to be addressed and corrected are agreed upon. There needs to be commitment from the employee, as well as the manager to help the employee towards improvement.

A performance improvement plan can often vary. The basic gist of a PIP includes the following elements.

Collaboration. The employer and employee can and should work together on the PIP. It can be a chance to make a positive change for all. Each side can provide input and communicate concerns.

Communication. Perhaps there are missed or misunderstood concerns from either or both sides. Are there personal problems that may be a part of the problem? Would time off provide a needed break for the employee? Is the employee not feeling challenged? Is there resentment being harboured over something or someone in the workplace? Communication from both parties is necessary, along with clear expectations on the required changes.

Compliment (Positivity). The PIP discussion should include more than just the issue(s) at hand. It is important for anyone to hear their positive attributes. All too often, it is easy to point out the negative and fail to consider how important it is to also include positive, constructive feedback. Tell the employee of the great things you notice about them.

Clarity. Provide clear and concise information. This includes clear details about dates, timelines, further training (whether on the job and/or on their own time) that may be required.

Consistent. Regular and ongoing reviews and feedback are provided to an employee. Constructive feedback (positive and negative) is provided regularly.

All sides (employee, employer, union) are fully aware of exactly what is expected, and all work toward improving.

Again, I can't be clear enough, this step is for the *same* problem or errors documented in steps one and two; it is *not* to be used for a new or different problem.

Once steps one and two have been exhausted, then, and only then, should this be considered.

If this step is the only alternative, please use some compassion. But remember that compassion should also be used *throughout* the progressive discipline process.

The conversations in every step should be upfront, genuine, and honest. Feedback, support, and encouragement should be ongoing. In most cases, the employee will understand and know if there is an issue with their work, and the majority of employees genuinely want to improve.

For example, upon meeting and discussing a PIP plan with Jane, her employer discovered that Jane had been harbouring resentment about being passed over for a promotion. What she was not aware of was that the other employee had both the experience and applicable education for that position. Her supervisor was not aware of Jane's desires to move to another position, or if she was interested in furthering her education toward advancement within the company.

In this situation, Jane was put on a PIP regarding her tardiness. The communication between her and her supervisor dramatically improved, and she was able to take online university courses toward another fulfilling position.

Step 4: Termination

Obviously, this is (and should be) a last resort.

It is critical that there is clear and concise documentation every step of the way. Every single step prior to and during this progressive discipline process is documented. If within a unionized environment, a union representative is permitted. As always, ensure compassion.

For example, Jane's attitude remained unchanged. Her abrasiveness toward her manager and co-worker was obvious, and her tardiness did not improve.

As a result, Jane and her union representative's presence were requested. A compassionate discussion was held wherein Jane was dismissed.

Fig. 14.4 provides a more descriptive illustration that might be easier to follow and understand.

As you can see, there may be more than one verbal warning or written warning. There is no hard-and-fast rule that there needs to be just one warning. The goal for all should be for the employee to continue to be employed.

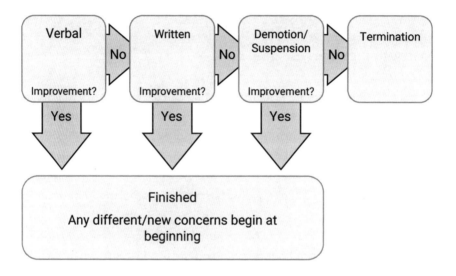

Figure 14.4: The progressive discipline flow chart.

Exceptions

Exceptions in the order of steps of progressive discipline may include:

- Unwillingness to follow health and safety standards
- Retaliation against an employee
- Corruption or bribery
- Sexual harassment

- Workplace violence
- Embezzlement or fraud
- Substance abuse
- *Major* mistakes on the job

There are notable situations whereby progressive discipline is needed and utilized. Used properly, progressive discipline is an effective tool to address problematic issues in the workplace.

However, the focus of this book is workplace harassment and bullying. With that, there are some in leadership positions who are incorrectly applying progressive discipline.

Mishandling progressive discipline may or may not be intentional. Regardless, it is essential anyone in a leadership position knows, learns, and understands what is and is not acceptable.

Improperly conducted progressive discipline (whether intentional or not) can be viewed as another bullying tactic.

I have witnessed and been aware of situations whereby this was also utilized as a tool to encourage employees to resign. This can be construed as constructive dismissal.

CHAPTER 15:
Non-Disclosure Agreements

Non-disclosure agreements (NDAs) in the workplace are also often referred to as "gagging clauses."

An NDA is a legally binding contract that a person signs to agree to keep information confidential. It is often used for company trade secrets that they want to keep from competitors. However, it has increasingly been utilized to silence employees who have left or are leaving a toxic workplace. In return, there is often a monetary payout.

It is absolutely shocking at the number of NDAs toxic environments will pay in attempts to hide their toxicity. The majority I've been aware of, speculative of, and heard of are often in larger businesses, including all levels of government. In Canada, this can be municipal, provincial (state), and federal. These can, and often do, add significant cost to taxpayers, shareholders, and others with a monetary interest in the business or government body. Toxic organizations often pay out multiple NDAs in a year, depending on their size, resulting in payouts of hundreds of thousands of dollars, if not more, in a given year, which can add significant costs to any business.

And what about accountability, especially when an NDA pertains to any level of government: Regional health authorities (RHAs), municipalities (including cities), the RCMP, police departments, and so on? As a taxpayer, I am dumbfounded at the volume of NDAs our government—municipal, provincial, and federal—have and continue to pay in order to silence those affected.

I applaud the Minister of Business in the UK for attempting to bring in legislation to address those utilizing NDAs to hide toxic environments. According to the UK government's website, the objectives for this legislation include:

- Clarity for victims on disclosing wrongdoing to the police, regulated health and care professionals, and legal professionals
- "[N]ot [tolerating] the use of NDAs to silence and intimidate victims to prevent them speaking out," as noted by Business Minister Kelly Tolhurst
- New legislation through the government's Good Work Plan to create a fairer workplace for all (Tolhurst & Mordaunt, 2019)

As the earlier points show, there are some organizations utilizing non-disclosures to silence victims of workplace bullying and/or harassment. Often, as a result, further employees are subjected to workplace harassment/bullying, and the organization's toxic culture continues to fester (NDAs: New laws to crack down on "gagging" clauses, 2019).

It is quite understandable as to why some choose to sign NDAs. Attempts to address toxic environments are often ignored or twisted around, and the person experiencing the abuse usually exits the organization one way or another. As we saw in *Boucher v Wal-Mart*, the employee may then have difficulty finding employment afterwards.

As we are all aware, there are always family and financial obligations. Sometimes, the bullied employee is the sole bread winner. With financial obligations, and needing to recoup and/or move ahead in life, the NDA provides financial incentives, which are often the motivating factors for employees, particularly former employees, to sign the NDA.

This was the case in Lucy Nichol's article, titled "I've signed two NDAs. Let's ban them so we can speak the truth about workplace bullying." Nichol, who signed two non-disclosures, states in her article,

> As somebody who has had to sign two NDAs to be compensated for the jobs I lost and the health implications I suffered due to workplace bullying, I feel passionately that the use of NDAs is wholly wrong. (2019)

The author makes numerous good points, including:

- The need for financial compensation.
- Cost of health implications suffered due to workplace bullying.
- Attempts to explain your situation to HR. In Lucy's situation, she attempted to advise HR of her stress and anxiety as a result of her workplace, with no results.
- Stress and anxiety over the possibility of having to go into a toxic workplace.
- Feeling helpless.
- Need for grievances (investigations) to be dealt with by external investigators to ensure objectivity.
- The inability of a person who signed an NDA to talk about their experience. Should a person even speak to a counsellor, this is breaking the contract. While client–patient confidentiality is normally in place, if it were inadvertently leaked out, this would pose possible legal consequences.
- Inaccurate picture as to how large the problem of workplace bullying is, whether at a given organization, or throughout the world. (Nichol, 2019)

Will the UK be successful in implanting the legislation proposed against NDAs? At the time of publishing, there appears to be no further progress.

Will others throughout the world follow suit? Will they enforce this legislation? How about the existing legislation many employers appear to circumvent regarding workplace bullying and/or harassment? Who will be tasked with ensuring it is all upheld?

Hopefully, other countries—along with their regions, counties, states, provinces, etc.—will see the importance and the need to ensure follow-up/through of such legislation(s).

CHAPTER 16:
Constructive Dismissal

Constructive dismissal is also referred to as disguised dismissal, constructive discharge, or constructive termination. It is a legal term that many find confusing. When first heard, particularly by a harassed employee, it can add further insult to injury.

Dismissal, to many, appears to suggest just that: dismissal. It contradicts the fact that the employee, as in *Boucher v Wal-Mart*, resigned.

Constructive dismissal describes situations where the employer has not directly fired the employee. Rather, the employer has failed to comply with the contract of employment in a major respect, unilaterally changed the terms of employment, or expressed a settled intention to do either, thus forcing the employee to quit. Constructive dismissal is sometimes called "disguised dismissal" or "quitting with cause" because it often occurs in situations where the employee is offered the alternative of leaving or of submitting to a unilateral and substantial alteration of a fundamental term or condition of their employment. Whether or not there has been a constructive dismissal is based on an objective view of the employer's conduct and not merely on the employee's perception of the situation (Constructive dismissal - 815-1-IPG-033, 2020).

Following is how I explain constructive dismissal for those unaware of it or confused about this terminology. With the word *constructive*, things change. An employer can constructively change the terms or conditions of the workplace in a variety of ways.

Examples of constructive changes (or constructive acts) can include bullying/harassment, duties removed that an employee previously held, failing to investigate a complaint, failing to properly investigate a complaint, disciplinary action (e.g., utilization of progressive discipline to rid themselves of an employee), retaliation against an employee (e.g., whistleblower), profanity, ridicule, and more.

These constructive acts then push the affected employee into feeling there is no other choice but to resign. This is why constructive dismissal is confusing.

Like some in leadership positions, some employees initially think they "voluntarily" left their positions when they resign. People with poor leadership skills falsely believe these constructive methods successfully and safely rid themselves (or the company) of an employee.

However, the changes to the terms or conditions of the employment are the contributing factor(s) to the resignation. These changes are normally substantial, and not agreed upon (accepted) by the employee. As a result, the employee resigns. This is constructive dismissal.

CHAPTER 17:
Working Toward Organizational Change

> "In periods where there is no leadership, society stands still. Progress occurs when courageous, skillful leaders seize the opportunity to change things for the better."
>
> —Harry Truman, former US President

Organizations with poor leadership, such as those discussed, can still progress. With skilled and courageous leaders, these organizations *can* change for the better.

A starting point can include a well-written and respectful workplace policy that is actually followed.

Respectful Workplace Policies

With the prevalence of workplace harassment and bullying, many organizations throughout the world are now required to have a policy in place that addresses how to deal with poor behaviour in the workplace. Properly written and followed respectful workplace policies can lead to a healthier workplace and aid in reducing investigations.

Often, the requirements within respectful workplace policies depend on legislation for the given area and its jurisdiction—federal or provincial/state. Many laws may also have requirements as to what should be included within a respectful workplace policy.

Tips and suggestions on respectful workplace policies from the Canadian Centre for Occupational Health and Safety (CCOHS) are included in the appendix.

While there are a number of templates for respectful workplace policies, tailoring one to your company is important. Know and understand your policy. Practise what you preach. Sending out emails promoting positivity is not enough.

- Model the behaviour that is expected and provide ongoing education and feedback on respectful workplace policies.
- Encourage all staff to report problematic behaviour.
- Deal with each situation, whether it is reported or not. Don't wait for a formal written complaint if you are aware of problematic behaviours or situations.
- Ensure confidentiality and that there is no retaliation.
- Provide a counselling/employee assistance program (EAP) for employees. Both those targeted and bullies can benefit from counselling services.
- Be supportive to all. All employees should feel safe to address their concerns.

All employees throughout an organization need to fully understand their policies, ensure they are compliant, and understand reporting processes. This may include training sessions to better understand and recognize bullying within the workplace, guidance on the respectful workplace policy within their organization, and review of their reporting processes.

Section 3
Investigations

"Condemnation without investigation
is the height of ignorance."

—Albert Einstein

CHAPTER 18:
Bullying Investigations in the Workplace

Conducting investigations into workplace bullying could easily be a book in itself. There are a wide variety of areas that can and should be covered. What constitutes a shoddy investigation, defining the scope of an investigation, how to conduct investigative interviews, and report writing are just a few topics surrounding investigations.

This section on investigations is short and sweet. The bulk of the book was to bring awareness of the pandemic of bullying within our workplaces. Due to the high incidence of leadership avoiding investigations, failing to conduct investigations, or running sham/unfair investigations, I felt the information included in this chapter needed to be provided to both employees and employers.

The quote at the beginning of section 3 from Albert Einstein is simple and articulate. It is easy to accuse, criticize, blame, censor, punish, reprimand, or ridicule.

A glimpse at the following survey, completed by Gary and Ruth Namie, verifies just that. While the statistics are older (2008), they provide startling statistics on bullying and harassment investigations within the workplace, whether poorly conducted or not conducted at all.

The Namies, founders of the Workplace Bullying Institute (WBI), surveyed 400 people, asking them what their employers did when they reported being bullied. The results are as follows:

- 1.7% conducted a fair investigation and protected the target with punitive measures against the bully.
- 6.2% conducted a fair investigation with punitive measures for the bully but no protection for the target.
- 8.7% conducted an unfair investigation with no punitive measure for the bully.
- 31% conducted an inadequate/unfair investigation with no punitive measures for the bully, but plenty for the target.
- 12.8% did nothing or ignored the problem with no consequences for anyone, bully or target.
- 15.7% did nothing, but retaliated against the target for reporting. Target remained employed.
- 24% of employers did nothing except fire the target.

Shocking statistics, aren't they? More recent statistics were just compiled by the Workplace Bullying Institute and were discussed at the end of chapter 5, including those targeted employees have a 67% chance of losing the jobs they loved for no legitimate reason.

Workplace investigations need to be unbiased, neutral, and fair. In "A Quick Guide for Conducting Workplace Investigations," Marshall states, "A key component of conducting a fair workplace investigation involves using an investigator who is neutral, unbiased, and who will be evenhanded with the parties and witnesses" (Marshall, 2019).

Unfortunately, this is where many organizations seem to continue to fail.

The Elgert v Home Hardware Investigation

Take, for example, the case of *Elgert v Home Hardware*. There were obviously a number of issues with this poorly conducted investigation. The investigator was biased, as he was a close and long-time friend of the owner, and he lacked training and experience in investigations. He was accusatory toward Elgert ("You know what you did") when Elgert asked what he was being accused of (Elgert v Home Hardware Stores Limited, 2011). He not only failed to interview Elgert, but also failed to interview other key witnesses, including those who signed a petition circulated in support of Elgert. The investigation appears to have lacked confidentiality. And, finally, the investigator's suggestion that he was one hundred per cent certain of Elgert's guilt showed a predetermined decision prior to the investigation.

Elgert was found to have been wrongfully dismissed. The sexual harassment accusations were determined to be false, and damages were awarded.

Shoddy or sham investigations have huge consequences for organizations. Damages awarded can be very costly. Then there are lawyer fees. In addition, employee morale can decline, employee loyalty often decreases, and customer loyalty may be diminished due to negative publicity. Potential future candidates may think twice before considering employment at any given organization that treats employees poorly, thus increasing recruitment and retention costs. As you can see, poorly conducted or sham investigations are costly, both in terms of money and a company's reputation.

Elements of an Effective Workplace Investigation

There are elements for effective workplace investigations. Knowing them is important for any organization.

According to Dr. David Yamada, "Education and policies are only the beginning. The next step, a much more difficult one, is to enforce policies relating to bullying by conducting genuine follow-up investigations and where necessary, assessing reprisals, when complaints arise" (2008).

When workplace investigations are required, they should:

- Be free of condemnation prior to investigation.

- Be impartial and unbiased.
- Be free of retaliation against the target and/or whistleblower.
- Ensure and provide (when needed) protection for whistleblowers or those targeted.
- Be conducted by someone trained and competent.
- Be confidential.

The interviewer, those interviewed, and anyone else involved must be aware of the need to ensure the confidentiality of the investigation. This can and may mean hiring a third party to conduct the investigation.

For anyone unsure of where to start with a workplace bullying/harassment investigation, the Association of Workplace Investigators (AWI) is one avenue. They have a large international database of members. They offer training and education programs about conducting impartial workplace investigations. Plus, they publish *Guiding Principles for Conducting Workplace Investigations* and *AWI Journal*.

> Founded in 2009, the Association of Workplace Investigators is a professional membership association for attorneys, human resource professionals, private investigators, and many others who conduct, manage, or have a professional interest in workplace investigations.
>
> Our mission is to promote and enhance the quality of impartial workplace investigations. (About the Association of Workplace Investigators, 2021)

Section 4
Parting Thoughts

Initially, it totally flabbergasted me (as well as numerous others I know) as to how poorly some organizations dealt with serious issues of workplace harassment/bullying. Why are they not following the applicable laws, or even their own policies? How can organizations treat their own employees this way? How can they destroy the lives and livelihoods of employees already dealing with harassment and bullying?

Learning as much as I could about bullying and harassment helped me to better understand the complexities of bullying and harassment within the workplace. Understanding the differences in leadership styles also helped. Hearing stories from others also affected assisted me in understanding just how widespread the problem is, and that I am not alone. Reading and understanding various case laws on different workplace bullying and harassment cases resounded with me more than I could have imagined. And ongoing education with human resources, mediation, and workplace investigations reassured me that some of the actions and behaviours by some in leadership positions were unacceptable.

All in all, knowledge really is power. With knowledge comes a better understanding. And with a better understanding, a greater awareness of what is and is not acceptable.

And, with that, there are also the implications for the affected organizations. Organizations need to understand and see the importance of recognizing and dealing with workplace bullying and harassment. Failing to address harassment and bullying concerns can result in a variety of negative factors, including:

- Higher turnover
- Higher stress levels
- Increased sick time
- Lower productivity
- Decreased profits

- Toxic environments
- Distrust within
- Payouts (e.g., NDAs)

This information makes it even more perplexing as to why any organization wouldn't proactively deal with harassment and bullying. Perhaps part of the problem is the need for a better understanding of workplace harassment and bullying. It is obvious that more knowledge and understanding regarding this often misunderstood and poorly handled pandemic—I call it a pandemic as it seems to be increasing and expanding throughout the world at an alarming rate—is essential to a healthy, productive workplace.

Coincidentally, while working and researching for this book, I came upon the article "Workplace bullying: The other epidemic" by Denise Koster (2020), who has spent 25 years working in the areas of workplace violence and harassment. Naturally, given the timing, subject matter, and appropriateness of titles, I felt it would be an added enhancement for this book. I am pleased to have the opportunity to share this insightful article in the appendix.

In many ways, this book also evolved much like an epidemic or pandemic. Had I not gone through the experiences I did, I would have had no idea how insidious workplace bullying and harassment actually are. While obviously not enjoyable, the experience changes your perceptions and views on the subject.

As with each bullying or harassment experience, working through the traumatic experience is different for everyone. Part of my recovery required anti-depressants, many sleepless nights, counselling, tears, and a quest to understand as much as I could about this serious subject.

Education was key. I forged on and finished my Payroll Compliance Practitioner (PCP) certificate, University Certificate in Human Relations and Labour Relations (UCHRLR), and Anatomy of Investigations and Mediations. And I spoke with numerous others affected by workplace harassment and bullying.

While every story was different, they were also similar. Workplace bullying and harassment changes a person. For each person I spoke to, their experience and trauma were shocking and painful, so painful that some do not make it through the experience. For those who do make it, their shock and disbelief (along with a multitude of other feelings) can fester for years. But despite the shock and disbelief, there are positives.

Positives of the experience are, thankfully, plentiful. A huge plus is the friendships forged with others affected by workplace harassment or bullying. I've developed a greater awareness of the positives in my life. I believe I have become a more understanding and compassionate person as a result of my experiences. This is particularly reflected in my feelings for so many others suffering workplace bullying or harassment.

Perhaps that is partly why I initially tried so hard not to include my experiences of bullying and harassment. I didn't want to be negative or complain. I knew I wasn't the only one. Speaking about experiences of bullying or harassment can and often sounds negative. But, in my effort not to do so, the initial draft was factual, fragmented, and (as noted by my editor) lacked much of my own words and voice. After the sting wore off, I have to admit I do appreciate the honesty.

As a result, countless additional hours were spent revamping this book. I truly had no idea just how much work it would require and how time-consuming this quest really was.

But, because I feel there is a need for the information within these pages, I forged on. Without the added information from so many others, both those included within the book and others who remain unnamed, this book would not have been possible.

This book is dedicated to all of those who:

- Are suffering from workplace harassment or bullying.
- Have gone through workplace harassment or bullying.
- Have allowed the inclusion of their articles or information.
- Are amazing people I have not only met, but also forged friendships with as a result.
- Want to better understand workplace bullying or harassment.
- Are committed to ensuring a safe and healthy workplace.

- Believed in me and this quest.

And last, but definitely not least, this book is dedicated to my family. If this book has been helpful, then my quest has been successful.

Appendix

Don't Rush to Judge Employees on Medical, Disability Leave

By Stuart Rudnar

This article was originally published by *The Lawyer's Daily* (www.thelawyersdaily.ca), part of LexisNexis Canada Inc., and is reprinted with the permission of the author and publisher.

There are some pieces of advice that I offer repeatedly to clients in a variety of contexts. One of my favourites: "Do not rush to judgment." Those knee-jerk, visceral or emotional reactions usually lead to bad decisions which can cost an organization dearly.

Often, this arises in the context of an employee that is on medical or disability leave. For many employers, having a worker on an extended leave is frustrating, as they have to try to run their business without knowing if or when the employee will return. And in many cases, there is suspicion that the employee is not really disabled and is milking the system. So, when the employer thinks they have caught the employee doing something that they shouldn't, they often rush to judgment and fire them. Unfortunately, this often costs them in the long run. Two common examples:

- The employer becomes aware of photos or videos of the employee engaging in physical activity while they claim to be medically unable to work; and

- The employer finds out that their employee on medical leave is taking vacation.

In the first example, the employer often feels they have just found the "smoking gun." After all, if this employee is medically unable to do their job, how can they be skiing, biking, carrying heavy packages while walking briskly through a parking lot, etc.? They rush to judgment and assume that this discovery entitles them to fire the "dishonest" employee.

Unfortunately, they rarely take the time to 1) make sure their suspicion is accurate and 2) assess whether it warrants dismissal before they terminate the employment relationship.

That was the case in *Winnipeg Regional Health Authority v Manitoba Association of Health Care Professionals*, a 2018 arbitration decision (Placeholder3). Roshni Tailor began working as a sonographer at the Winnipeg Health Sciences Centre in the fall of 2010. Over the years, she suffered multiple repetitive strain injuries to her wrists and elbow. Each time, she would take time off work to recover and then return.

In January 2017, Tailor was off duty when she fell and broke her wrist while performing a cultural dance routine. As a result, she was unable to work and received short-term disability benefits until the end of March. In April, she was deemed able to return to work on a graduated basis, with restrictions including no pushing, pulling, gripping (or grasping) with her right upper extremities.

Unfortunately, these limitations effectively precluded Tailor from working as a sonographer and, since there were no other duties she could assume, she remained on leave. Since the employer was unable to accommodate Tailor with modified duties, she eventually went on long-term disability (LTD).

Tailor started a reconditioning program in September 2017 but had to stop due to the pain it caused to her neck and back. At that point, the employer requested an independent medical examination, which Tailor underwent and that resulted in a recommendation that she participate in a lighter reconditioning program.

Tailor did return to work in February 2018, on a graduated basis. However, on Feb. 26, she reported that she was experiencing pain in her wrist, neck and back. Her shifts were reduced and there was a recommendation that she only perform scans that were shorter and less physically demanding, with breaks between each one.

Things went off the rails in May when videos of Tailor doing cultural dancing and running surfaced. The LTD insurer contacted Tailor and advised that it was discontinuing her benefits as the videos suggested that she was no longer totally disabled. Tailor was directed to remain off work pending the outcome of an investigation into her condition. Notably, she was not paid while off work.

At the next meeting, the employer delivered a termination letter, stating that they could not trust Tailor in light of the fact that she was engaging in this physical activity while claiming to be physically unable to work.

Not surprisingly, Tailor grieved the dismissal. And while it may surprise some, she was successful. The arbitrator agreed that the videos of Tailor dancing strongly suggested that she was not suffering pain or impairment. Notably, a comparison of videos before and after the injury showed little change. However, the arbitrator went on to find that there was a significant difference between the physical requirements of a sonographer and the physical activity demonstrated in the videos.

According to the arbitrator, Kristin Gibson, there was insufficient evidence to require an explanation from Tailor: "... I do not feel able to conclude without medical evidence that there is the required degree of inconsistency to shift the onus to her."

Among other things, the arbitrator took note of the fact that Tailor had advised the people running the reconditioning program about the resumption of her dancing, so there was no dishonesty or effort to hide what she was doing.

Ultimately, Tailor was reinstated with full back pay.

This happens every now and then: an employer thinks they have a "gotcha" moment where they have caught an employee lying and cheating the system. They then rush to judgment without getting proper legal advice or assessing the case objectively.

It is important to remember that someone who is "medically unable to work" does not necessarily have to remain in bed or at home, immobile, all day. Like Tailor, the individual may be able to engage in physical activity, but not the physical activities that form part of their duties. Similarly, an employee suffering from anxiety or depression which prevents them from working may be able to go skiing or play hockey with their kids.

The bottom line: Some employees do cheat the system. If there is evidence to support that, action most certainly should be taken. But just because someone is deemed to be medically unable to do their job does not necessarily mean they cannot engage in any physical activity. So be careful about jumping to conclusions.

Similarly, I have seen employers vehemently insist that a worker on medical leave be fired because they went on vacation while on leave. While a leave should not be used in order to take a vacation, there is nothing inherently wrong with an employee who is on a legitimate medical leave taking a vacation. Again, considering the situation objectively and getting legal advice will help employers in those situations avoid a costly misstep.

Unfortunately, our firm is often only brought in after the fact, to help the employer minimize the damage.

Stuart Rudner is a leading Canadian employment lawyer and mediator at Rudner Law. He is the author of *You're Fired! Just Cause for Dismissal in Canada.*

Addressing the Bystander Effect in the Workplace

By Heather Ikin, Organisational Psychologist

Originally published January 5, 2015; reprinted with permission.

Human behaviour is an interesting phenomenon. As a Psychologist, I often observe the actions of others and reflect on why it is we behave and respond to the world in the ways that we do.

A few days ago a Melbourne colleague sent me a link to an interesting article published in The Age on January 29th. An incident had occurred at Caulfield Railway Station involving a young man in significant distress and demonstrating at-risk behaviour. A witness interviewed for this news article reported that whilst she watched this situation unfold, she felt that if no one intervened this young man would jump onto the track.

At the request of one bystander for help, she approached and spoke to the young man until emergency services arrived. This witness, a former nurse, reported that she was appalled by the lack of intervention by some 40 other individuals waiting on the platform.

Reflecting on the article, I actually did not feel surprised at the lack of action from those at the station.

If it was you in this situation, how would you respond?

Interestingly, a lot of research has been conducted on such situations and how people respond to dangerous or traumatic events. Such research has demonstrated that in these situations, we are often reluctant to intervene and offer assistance to a victim or at-risk individual, and that the greater the number of bystanders, the less likely it is that any one individual will involve themselves in the situation. This is often referred to as the "Bystander Effect."

In my experience as a consultant working with organisations, we see similar effects in response to occupational violence, workplace bullying, harassment, and discrimination. Whilst many employees may witness or even experience inappropriate and harmful behaviours and acts in the workplace, many fail to intervene.

So why does this phenomenon occur? Is it because we lack compassion or empathy, that we are immune to the painful experiences of others?

As humans, we are hard wired to avoid threatening situations. When we observe such behaviour in others, we exercise high degrees of caution due to feelings of uncertainty and inability to predict another's behaviour. The Bystander Effect can occur as a result of this desire to avoid harm, whilst also being able to rationalise the decision not to intervene by diffusing responsibility to others. The more witnesses the more people to assign the responsibility to intervene. For many of those individuals at Caulfield Railway Station, they would have been much more likely to take action had they been the only other person present.

It is important for organisations to consider such effects of behaviour and psychology in the workplace. In order to eliminate harmful behaviour and mitigate the risks associated with experiencing violence, bullying, harassment or discrimination at work, employers should take action to encourage workers to take action.

What can organisations do to support employees to intervene or address harmful and at-risk behaviour when it occurs?

- Provide employees and managers with training on how to respond to occupational violence and workplace bullying and role model desired behaviours as a part of your health, safety and wellbeing strategy

- Ensure all employees and managers are aware of the appropriate processes and procedures for responding to emergency situations, including contact details for post incident support such as employee assistance program providers and services such as Lifeline

- Establish a network of support officers that have received adequate training in mental health first aid and basic counselling skills
- Conduct awareness sessions and make information available to employees on mental health in the workplace
- Develop a strong culture of health, safety and wellbeing across your workforce and encourage employee commitment to taking action to ensure a safe workplace for all

By implementing these strategies, employers can ensure they fulfill their duty of care to both those in distress and to those who may also me impacted by their behaviour.

Workplace Bullying: The Other Epidemic

By: Denise Koster, Koster Consulting & Associates

Originally published by *The Lawyer's Daily*, June 29, 2020; reprinted with permission.

During and following the COVID-19 pandemic, there is a critical need for employers to be even more vigilant regarding their occupational health and safety responsibilities. For the past few months, workplace bullies and harassers have been methodically developing new and sophisticated tactics to virtually and digitally eliminate their target from the workplace.

After 25 years of working in the field of workplace violence and harassment, I know first-hand the devastating consequences of workplace bullying, both for individuals and the organizations that employ them. There are significant costs associated with what I see as an epidemic, including productivity drops, stress leaves and staff turnover. Research shows that harassed and bullied employees frequently develop mental health problems, such as anxiety, costing employers $20 billion a year, according to estimates from the Mental Health Commission of Canada.

In December 2019, seven executives of a French telecom company were convicted and jailed following a series of suicides by employees, reports *Talent Canada* magazine, noting that the managers attempted to reduce overhead through a harassment campaign designed to encourage resignations.

Several years ago, a man I encountered during the course of a workplace investigation was bullied at work to the point where he deliberately drove his car into a tree and had to be hospitalized for his injuries. He admitted to me that although he did not want to kill himself, he wanted to ensure that he "messed myself up enough" so that he could take a few months off. In his mind, the physical pain caused by the accident was a better option than the mental agony he was forced to endure as a result of a systemic campaign of workplace bullying. Although this employee's bully hid behind an office wall to torment his subordinate, the detrimental psychological effects on the target were no different than present-day bullies concealing themselves by the protective shield of home offices and computer screens.

Over the past decade, instances of cyber-bullying have escalated with online harassment emerging as a preferred path for many bullies to terrorize their victims. With flexibility in work schedules and a lack of established in-house rules such as stringent meeting etiquette, harassers are now able to gain a false sense of security based on anonymity. This is a direct outcome of employers being consumed with technical and equipment issues while they disregard or minimize interpersonal differences or complaints of internal workplace bullying and harassment.

Despite the fact that self-empowerment through personal validation is a critical survival tool for targets of workplace discrimination and harassment, there is a thin line between freedom of speech and false claims or malicious defamatory comments made about management. Moreover, an emerging trend facing employers is the increasing number of blogs, social media posts and professional platforms that invite employees to openly criticize their employers. Publicly voicing dissatisfaction—ranging from a personal opinion on a standard policy to a personal judgment regarding how an employer is handling a pandemic-related procedure such as the gradual return-to-work process—is now commonplace.

The bystander effect, sometimes called "Genovese Syndrome," following Kitty Genovese's 1964 murder in Queens, New York, is a conscious decision that employers make to not intervene or become involved in online displays of incivility, disrespect or aggressive behavior. It is critical for employers to immediately update, implement and enforce existing social networking and cyber-bullying policies to address the organizational mob mentality or conscious silence that is emerging in workplaces. Working remotely does not decrease an employee's obligation to report breaches in labour laws or allow them to choose neutrality as an option.

Workplace violence and harassment investigations need to be carried out vigilantly by highly trained and skilled investigators. Best practices must be applied swiftly and with due diligence, reflecting ever changing workplace settings. Any delay in accountability or adapting a willful blindness approach will increase the level of group complacency and, in the end, risk liability for employers.

What Can an Employer Do?

Excerpt from the *Violence in the Workplace Prevention Guide*

https://www.ccohs.ca/products/publications/violence.html

By the Canadian Centre for Occupational Health and Safety

Reproduced with permission of the CCOHS, 2020.

The most important component of any workplace prevention program is management commitment. Management commitment is best communicated in a written policy. Since bullying is a form of violence in the workplace, employers may wish to write a comprehensive policy that covers a range of incidents (from bullying and harassment to physical violence).

A workplace violence prevention program must:

- Be developed by management and employee representatives
- Apply to management, employee's, clients, independent contractors and anyone who has a relationship with your company
- Define what you mean by workplace bullying (or harassment or violence) in precise, concrete language
- Provide clear examples of unacceptable behaviour and working conditions
- State in clear terms your organization's view toward workplace bullying and its commitment to the prevention of workplace bullying
- Precisely state the consequences of making threats or committing acts

- Outline the process by which preventive measures will be developed
- Encourage reporting of all incidents of bullying or other forms of workplace violence
- Outline the confidential process by which employees can report incidents and to whom
- Assure no reprisals will be made against reporting employees
- Outline the procedures for investigating and resolving complaints
- Describe how information about potential risks of bullying/violence will be communicated to employees
- Make a commitment to provide support services to victims
- Offer a confidential Employee Assistance Program (EAP) to allow employees with personal problems to seek help
- Make a commitment to fulfill the prevention training needs of different levels of personnel within the organization
- Make a commitment to monitor and regularly review the policy
- State applicable regulatory requirements, where possible

A Quick Guide for Conducting Workplace Investigations

An effective, fair investigation after workplace misconduct or incidents can go a long way towards reducing liability for employers.

By Nathaniel Marshall

Originally published in *Canadian Employment Law Today*, May 1, 2019, by Key Media; reprinted with permission.

> *Despite legislation mandating that investigations must be undertaken, there are no hard-and-fast rules on how to conduct a proper workplace investigation. As a result, many employers continue to conduct investigations that may not withstand legal scrutiny. Here you can find some key legal principles and best practices for conducting effective workplace investigations.*

Workplace investigations are becoming increasingly prominent in today's workplaces. In part, this is due to fairly recent legislative changes that require employers to conduct workplace investigations in certain circumstances. Employers have also recognized the benefits of conducting investigations prior to administering discipline, to identify issues with workplace morale, and to highlight areas for improvement within their workplace culture. Additionally, in certain circumstances, properly conducted workplace investigations can be effective tools to mitigate the risks associated with litigation or arbitration.

It's all about fairness

Employers have a legal obligation to fairly and impartially conduct workplace investigations, although determining what is fair will vary with the circumstances. A key component of conducting a fair workplace investigation involves using an investigator who is neutral, unbiased, and who will be even-handed with the parties and witnesses.

Investigations must also be conducted in a timely manner. This affords fairness to both the parties by avoiding undue delay because the sooner an investigation is completed, the sooner the employer can act. Proceeding expeditiously also helps produce a better-quality investigation, as memories and recollections rarely improve over time.

Employers should also be cognizant of whether it may be prudent to remove an employee from the workplace during the investigation process. Tensions and emotions often run high as the process unfolds, and in order to ensure fairness for all parties, it may be appropriate for the complainant or respondent to be placed on a paid leave or offered modified duties while the investigation is underway.

Understanding the purpose

It is essential to understand the purpose for which the investigation is being conducted. It could be in response to a legal obligation, because the employer received a complaint regarding an alleged breach of company policy, to determine if there are grounds to levy discipline, or to assist in identifying and resolving larger issues with the workplace culture. Ultimately, there are a myriad of reasons why an employer may need to investigate and understanding its purpose will often dictate the type of investigation that is appropriate in the circumstances.

Identifying the investigator

Depending on the purpose of the investigation, it may be advisable for the employer to conduct the investigation internally. However, while internal investigators may be suitable for routine and straightforward investigations, they may lack an ability to be impartial or deal with complex factual and legal issues. Although they can be more costly, retaining external investigators allows employers to select someone with the necessary skills and experience to properly conduct the investigation. Because they are not regularly employed in the workplace, external investigators are also less likely to present issues with impartiality.

An additional consideration the employer will want to keep in mind is whether it would like, or need, the investigation to be privileged. In some circumstances—though there is no guarantee of ensuring privilege—that can be accomplished by retaining an external investigator.

Defining the scope

Regardless of whether an internal or external investigator is conducting the investigation, the employer should establish specific scope around the investigation—such as its mandate, the timeline, whether the investigator has only been retained to perform fact-finding alone, or if the investigator should be tasked with providing recommendations.

It is not uncommon for issues to arise throughout an investigation. To the extent possible, the employer should indicate whether the investigator should address any additional complaints or cross-complaints beyond those initially identified, or if conducting a separate investigation is preferable. When defining the scope of the investigation, both the employer and investigator must have a clear understanding of the investigator's role. When using external counsel, this role should be spelled out in the retainer agreement.

Maintaining confidentiality

At the outset of every interview whether with the parties or witnesses, the best practice is to outline the investigative process and emphasize that all parties and witnesses are expected to maintain confidentiality over their participation in the investigation. Maintaining confidentiality is crucial to conducting an effective workplace investigation, as it helps preclude having the process undermined by gossip and collusion. Further, the limits of such confidentiality should also be communicated to all persons involved. It is also prudent to reiterate the confidentiality obligation at the conclusion of each interview.

Interviewing witnesses and assessing credibility

After reviewing any applicable workplace policies and complaint documents, the first interview to be conducted is typically with the complainant. This is the investigator's opportunity to get a complete picture of the issues by hearing the who, what, when, where, and why. The complainant should also be encouraged to provide any relevant documents to the investigator at this time. Additionally, the investigator will want to elicit any relevant contextual information, including the identity of any witnesses that should be interviewed.

After meeting with the complainant, the best practice is to distill the allegations into a complaint document and to provide it to the respondent in advance of their interview. The hallmark of procedural fairness in this context is for the respondent to know the allegations [against] him or her, and to have the opportunity to respond. Accordingly, it is imperative that the respondent have all allegations put to her for comment. The respondent is typically interviewed after the complainant and after they have had a reasonable opportunity to formulate a response.

The investigator will then want to meet with all witnesses with relevant information. After meeting with the witnesses, the investigator should consider if a follow-up with either party is necessary to fill in any gaps or to gather a more complete understanding of the facts.

Bear in mind that preparation is key and, where possible, the investigator should apprise themselves of all relevant facts and information to prepare questions in advance of conducting an interview.

Although it may not be practicable to always conduct interviews face-to-face, the investigator's findings will always involve an assessment of credibility. By conducting interviews in person, investigators are better suited to assess credibility by observing the parties, determining the appropriate questions, and testing competing or alternate narratives. A proper assessment of credibility is the foundation to an effective investigation.

Building the paper trail

A competent investigator keeps a well-documented paper trail of each step of the investigation. This includes establishing an investigation plan, taking detailed notes of all interviews, providing the witnesses the opportunity to review their notes to ensure accuracy, and having them sign off to confirm the same.

The investigator will want to preserve all documentary evidence obtained during the investigation to be reviewed while drafting the report and to support the ultimate findings and process, should either be challenged.

Preparing the report

In most cases, investigators are tasked with preparing a written report of their findings. The report sets out whether each allegation has been proven on the balance of probabilities, or, put another way, whether it is more likely than not that each allegation is true. In making this determination, the written investigation report should outline: the summary of the complaint or allegations; the investigative authority and process; an assessment of credibility; relevant contextual information; legal and policy framework; a summary of the evidence and findings; and the investigator's conclusions or recommendations, where part of the investigation's scope.

Deciding who gets what

Given the importance of maintaining confidentiality, and in some cases privilege, typically only the persons tasked with making a final decision on discipline flowing from an investigation, if any, should be provided with the investigation report. It is generally sufficient if the complainant and respondent are provided with a summary of the report; however, the employer should also keep any legal obligations regarding mandatory disclosure in mind—such as with workplace harassment—and consider if any other individuals should be informed of the results.

An effective workplace investigation can limit an employer's exposure to liabilities, damages and reputational harm. Although the above highlights some best practices that employers should keep it in mind when conducting workplace investigations, it is always best to seek independent legal advice with respect to every specific situation.

Nathaniel Marshall is an associate lawyer with Turnpenney Milne LLP, practicing in all areas of employment and labour law. For more information, visit turnpenneymilne.ca.

Time's Up for Toxic Workplaces

I invite you to read the June 2020 article "Time's up for toxic workplaces," by Manuela Priesemuth. It discusses abusive bosses and how the behaviour can spread throughout the given organizations.

This article speaks volumes to the importance of dealing with this behaviour. And, if it is left unchecked, it can quickly and easily manifest into a toxic environment.

It reinforces the importance of a respectful workplace culture for all. Priesemuth's article is available at https://hbr.org/2020/06/times-up-for-toxic-workplaces.

Human Rights Tribunals

BC Human Rights Commission
https://bchumanrights.ca/

Alberta Human Rights Commission
https://albertahumanrights.ab.ca

Saskatchewan Human Rights Commission
https://saskatchewanhumanrights.ca/

Manitoba Human Rights Commission
http://www.manitobahumanrights.ca/v1/

Ontario Human Rights Commission
http://www.ohrc.on.ca/en

Québec, Commission des droits de la personne et des droits de la jeunesse
https://www.cdpdj.qc.ca/en

New Brunswick Human Rights Commission
https://www2.gnb.ca/content/gnb/en/departments/nbhrc.html

Nova Scotia Human Rights Commission
https://humanrights.novascotia.ca/s

Prince Edward Island Human Rights Commission
https://www.peihumanrights.ca/

Newfoundland and Labrador Human Rights Commission
https://thinkhumanrights.ca

Yukon Human Rights Commission
https://thinkhumanrights.ca

Northwest Territories Human Rights Commission
https://nwthumanrights.ca/

Nunavut Human Rights Tribunal
http://www.nhrt.ca/

References

"I shouldn't be telling you this, but...": Court rules sharing confidential information is just cause for termination. (2018, March 22). Retrieved May 14, 2021, from Fasken: https://www.fasken.com/en/knowledge/2018/03/hr-space-court-rules-sharing-confidential-information-is-just-cause-for-termination/

About the Association of Workplace Investigators. (2021). Retrieved May 11, 2021, from Assocation of Workplace Investigators: https://www.awi.org/page/about_AWI

Badzmierowski, B. (2016). *The difference between school bullying and workplace bullying.* Retrieved May 11, 2021, from Crisis Prevention Institute: https://www.crisisprevention.com/en-CA/Blog/School-Bullying-Workplace-Bullying

Bardal v Globe & Mail Ltd., 294 (ON SC 1960). Retrieved May 14, 2021, from https://canlii.ca/t/gghxf

Barghout, C., & Levasseur, J. (2019a, October 9). *Brandon police investigate overdose death at home of top bureaucrat.* Retrieved May 11, 2021, from CBC: https://www.cbc.ca/news/canada/manitoba/brandon-cao-home-death-police-investigation-1.5314133

Barghout, C., & Levasseur, J. (2019b, October 17). *Convicted criminals were once believed to be living at Rod Sage's home, documents show.* Retrieved May 14, 2021, from CBC News: https://www.cbc.ca/news/canada/manitoba/rod-sage-brandon-city-manager-christine-mitchell-heroin-overdose-1.5320993

Bell, D. (2017, February 21). *13 Calgary police members file bullying complaints urging cultural, leadership changes.* Retrieved May 11, 2021, from CBC Calgary: https://www.cbc.ca/news/canada/calgary/cps-complaints-13-members-1.3992227

Boucher v Wal-Mart Canada Corp., 419 (ONCA 2014). Retrieved May 14, 2021, from https://canlii.ca/t/g6xvb

Bridges, A. (2018a, March 25). *The doc project: Her husband took his own life after he was bullied on the job.* Retrieved May 14, 2021, from CBC Radio: https://www.cbc.ca/radio/docproject/the-grader-operator-s-widow-1.4647084/her-husband-took-his-own-life-after-he-was-bullied-on-the-job-1.4647320

Bridges, A. (2018b, February 5). *Workers' Compensation Board Attributes Suicide of Sask. Man to his Employment.* Retrieved May 11, 2021, from CBC Saskatchewan: https://www.cbc.ca/news/canada/saskatchewan/workers-compensation-suicide-vawn-saskatchewan-robert-duhaime-1.4519486

British Columbia (Public Service Employee Relations Commission) v BCGSEU, 652 3 SCR 3 (SCC 1999). Retrieved May 14, 2021, from https://canlii.ca/t/1fqk1

British Columbia (Public Service Employee Relations Commission) v British Columbia Government Service Employees' Union. (2019, April 24). Retrieved May 11, 2021, from Wikipedia: https://en.wikipedia.org/wiki/British_Columbia_(Public_Service_Employee_Relations_Commission)_v_British_Columbia_Government_Service_Employees%27_Union

Bureaucracy. (2021). Retrieved May 11, 2021, from Cambridge Dictionary: https://dictionary.cambridge.org/dictionary/english/bureaucracy

Canadian Centre for Occupational Health and Safety. (2021, May 11). *Bullying in the workplace.* Retrieved May 11, 2021, from OSH answers fact sheets: https://www.ccohs.ca/oshanswers/psychosocial/bullying.html

Carlin, D. (2018, October 18). *Democratic, authoritarian, laissez-faire: What type of leader are you?* Retrieved May 14, 2021, from Forbes: https://www.forbes.com/sites/davidcarlin/2019/1

Complex post-traumatic stress disorder. (2021, May 1). Retrieved May 11, 2021, from Wikipedia: https://en.wikipedia.org/wiki/Complex_post-traumatic_stress_disorder

Constructive dismissal - 815-1-IPG-033. (2020, September 1). Retrieved from Government of Canada: https://www.canada.ca/en/employment-social-development/programs/laws-regulations/labour/interpretations-policies/constructive-dismissal.html

Cook, D. (2020a, February 6). *'I hoped for a better result:' Fear of speaking up, lack of confidence in leadership highlight city employee survey*. Retrieved from

Edmonton Journal: https://edmontonjournal.com/news/local-news/city-releases-latest-employee-survey-results

Cook, D. (2020b, October 22). *"This is clearly problematic": Most City of Edmonton employees not speaking up about discrimination or inappropriate behaviour, workplace survey highlights.* Retrieved from Edmonton Journal: https://edmontonjournal.com/news/local-news/city-of-edmonton-workforce-survey-results

DARVO. (2021, April 11). Retrieved May 11, 2021, from Wikipedia: https://en.wikipedia.org/wiki/DARVO

Dawson v FAG Bearings Ltd., 55459 (ON SC 2008). Retrieved May 14, 2021, from https://canlii.ca/t/21c13

Definition of "autocratic ladership". (n.d.). Retrieved May 11, 2021, from The Economic Times: https://economictimes.indiatimes.com/definition/autocratic-leadership

Difference between gossip and rumor. (2018, February 2). Retrieved May 11, 2021, from Difference between similar terms & objects: https://differencebetweenz.com/difference-between-gossip-and-rumor/

Elgert v Home Hardware Stores Limited, 112 (ABCA 2011). Retrieved May 14, 2021, from https://canlii.ca/t/fmhdh

Freyd, J. J. (1997, Februrary). II: Violations of power, adaptive blindness, and betrayal trauma theory. *Feminism & Psychology, 7*(1), 22–32.

Freyd, J. J. (2021). *Biography.* Retrieved May 14, 2021, from Jennifer J. Freyd, PhD: https://www.jjfreyd.com/bio

Gerster, J. (2020, February 10). *Federal Court certifies $1.1B RCMP bullying, harassment class action.* Retrieved May 14, 2021, from Global News: https://globalnews.ca/news/6488391/rcmp-bullying-harassment/

Gillman v Saan Stories Ltd., 6202 (AB QB 1992). Retrieved May 14, 2021, from https://canlii.ca/t/28nsd

Greenwood v Canada, 119 (FC 2020). Retrieved May 14, 2021, from https://canlii.ca/t/j4vm8

Griffin v Dell Canada Inc., 3557 (ON SC 2009). Retrieved May 14, 2021, from https://canlii.ca/t/22bn5

Heidenreich, P. (2019, January 24). *More City of Edmonton employees feel harassed, discriminated against; citizens increasingly part of problem: report.* Retrieved May 11, 2021, from

Global News: https://globalnews.ca/news/4886433/edmonton-city-employees-harassment-discrimination-2018/

Honda Canada Inc. v Keays, 39 2 SCR 362 (SCC 2008). Retrieved May 14, 2021, from https://canlii.ca/t/1z469

Huizen, J. (2020, July 14). *What is gaslighting?* Retrieved May 14, 2021, from Medical News Today: https://www.medicalnewstoday.com/articles/gaslighting

Human rights in Canada. (2020, November 5). Retrieved May 14, 2021, from Canadian Human Rights Commission: https://www.chrc-ccdp.gc.ca/en/about-human-rights/human-rights-canada

Ikin, H. (n.d.). *Addressing the bystander effect in the workplace.* Retrieved May 14, 2021, from Optimise Consulting: https://www.tmsconsulting.com.au/blog/addressing-the-bystander-effect-in-the-workplace/

Is it harassment? A tool to guide employees. (2015, August 21). Retrieved May 14, 2021, from Covernment of Canada: https://www.canada.ca/en/government/publicservice/wellness-inclusion-diversity-public-service/harassment-conflict-resolution/harassment-tool-employees.html

Juneja, P. (2021). *Strategic leadership: Definition and aualities of a strategic leader.* Retrieved May 14, 2021, from Management Study Guide: https://www.managementstudyguide.com/strategic-leadership.htm

Kageyama, Y. (2019, November 19). *Toyota worker's suicide ruled work-related after constant harassment from his boss.* Retrieved May 11, 2021, from The Globe & Mail: https://www.theglobeandmail.com/business/international-business/asia-pacific-business/article-toyota-workers-suicide-ruled-work-related-after-constant-harassment/

Karmel v Calgary Jewish Academy, 731 (ABQB 2015). Retrieved May 14, 2021, from https://canlii.ca/t/gm78f

Koster, D. (2020, June 29). *Workplace bullying: The other epidemic.* Retrieved May 11, 2021, from The Lawyer's Daily: https://www.thelawyersdaily.ca/articles/19838/workplace-bullying-the-other-epidemic

Laissez-faire leadership: Definition, tips and examples. (2021, February 11). Retrieved May 14, 2021, from Indeed career guide: https://www.indeed.com/career-advice/career-development/laissez-faire-leadership

Lalonde v Sena Solid Waste Holdings Inc., 374 (ABQB 2017). Retrieved May 14, 2021, from https://canlii.ca/t/h492z

Lee, S. (2020, July 28). *What is coaching leadership.* Retrieved May 14, 2021, from Torch: Digital learning + leadership + mentorship: https://torch.io/blog/what-is-coaching-leadership/

Marshall, N. (2019, May 1). *A quick guide for conducting workplace investigations*. Retrieved May 14, 2021, from Canadian Employment Law Today: https://www.hrreporter.com/employment-law/news/a-quick-guide-for-conducting-workplace-investigations/315946

Minkin, R. (2013, July 8). Co-worker's Facebook comments discriminatory, violate Ontario Human Rights Code. *Canadian HR Reporter*. Retrieved May 14, 2021, from https://www.hrreporter.com/employment-law/news/co-workers-facebook-comments-discriminatory-violate-ontario-human-rights-code/307672

Musgrave v Levesque Securities Inc., 50 CCEL (2d) 59 (NSSC 2000).

NDAs: New laws to crack down on "gagging" clauses. (2019, July 21). Retrieved from BBC News: https://www.bbc.com/news/uk-49060456

Nepotism. (2021). Retrieved May 14, 2021, from Open Education Sociology Dictionary: https://sociologydictionary.org/nepotism/

Neumeister, L. (2018, June 1). *Lawsuit makes new rape allegation against Harvey Weinstein*. Retrieved May 11, 2021, from CTV News: https://www.ctvnews.ca/entertainment/lawsuit-makes-new-rape-allegation-against-harvey-weinstein-1.3955547

Nichol, L. (2019, November 11). *I've signed two NDAs. Let's ban them so we can speak the truth about workplace bullying*. Retrieved May 14, 2021, from Independent: https://www.independent.co.uk/voices/anti-bullying-week-non-disclosure-agreements-workplace-silence-ndas-a9198861.html

Nossiter, A. (2019, December 19). *3 French executives convicted in suicides of 35 workers*. Retrieved May 11, 2021, from The New York Times: https://www.nytimes.com/2019/12/20/world/europe/france-telecom-suicides.html

Ormondi, V. (2019, December 31). *Three French executives convicted in the suicides of 35 Workers*. Retrieved May 11, 2021, from Your Black World: https://yourblackworld.net/2019/12/31/three-french-executives-convicted-in-the-suicides-of-35-workers/

Perez-Moreno v Kulczyski, 1974 (HRTO 2013). Retrieved May 14, 2021, from https://www.queensu.ca/humanrights/hrlg/meeting-headlines/meeting-13/perez

Pilon v Peugeot Canada Ltd., 1631 (ON SC 1980). Retrieved May 14, 2021, from https://canlii.ca/t/g1hcb

Province of Manitoba | v1. (2020, December 10). Retrieved May 11, 2021, from The Manitoba Human Rights Commission: https://manitobahumanrights.ca/v1/

Riegel, D. G. (2018, October 12). *Stop complaining about your colleagues behind their backs*. Retrieved May 14, 2021, from Harvard Business Review: https://hbr.org/2018/10/stop-complaining-about-your-colleagues-behind-their-backs

Rivera, J. (2018, July 11). *What is negligent retention?* Retrieved May 14, 2021, from LegalMatch: https://www.legalmatch.com/law-library/article/negligent-retention-lawyers.html

Roumeliotis, I. (2014, June 12). *"Workplace bullying: The silent epidemic.* Retrieved May 14, 2021, from CBC News: https://www.cbc.ca/news/business/workplace-bullying-a-major-concern-in-canada-says-woman-who-sued-wal-mart-1.2673109

Rubin, J. (2014, May 8). *B.C. bank botches investigation*. Retrieved May 11, 2021, from RubinThomlinson LLP: https://rubinthomlinson.com/bc-bank-botches-investigation/

Saint-Cyr, Y., & Moradi, A. Z. (2018, September 20). *Confidentiality breach can be just cause for termination*. Retrieved May 14, 2021, from Slaw: http://www.slaw.ca/2018/09/20/confidentiality-breach-can-be-just-cause-for-termination/

Sales, F., & Holak, B. (2021). *Definition: Strategic leadership*. Retrieved May 14, 2021, from TechTarget: https://searchcio.techtarget.com/definition/strategic-leadership

Scapegoating. (2021, February 28). Retrieved May 11, 2021, from Wikipedia: https://en.wikipedia.org/wiki/Scapegoating

Simons, P. (2017, November 18). *Paula Simons: City of Edmonton's broken workplace culture creates toxic waste*. Retrieved May 11, 2021, from Edmonton Journal: https://edmontonjournal.com/opinion/columnists/paula-simons-city-of-edmontons-broken-workplace-culture-creates-toxic-waste

Snell, J. (2021, February 19). *City's largest union lashes out at Bowman over Mayor's call to tackle racism*. Retrieved May 14, 2021, from Winnipeg Sun: https://winnipegsun.com/news/news-news/citys-largest-union-lashes-out-at-bowman-over-mayors-call-to-tackle-racism

Somos, C. (2021, January 4). *Growing list of Canadian politicians caught travelling abroad despite pandemic*. Retrieved May 11, 2021, from CTV News: https://www.ctvnews.ca/politics/growing-list-of-canadian-politicians-caught-travelling-abroad-despite-pandem

Supreme Court of Canada. (1997, October 30). *Wallace v. United Grain Growers Ltd.* Retrieved May 14, 2021, from Supreme Court Judgments: https://decisions.scc-csc.ca/scc-csc/scc-csc/en/item/1557/index.do

Taylor, C. M., Cornelius, C. J., & Colvin, K. (2014). Visionary leadership and its relationship to organizational effectiveness. *Leadership & Organizational Development Journal, 35*(6), 566-583. doi:10.1108/LODJ-10-2012-0130

The doc project: The grader operator's widow. (2018, May 18). Retrieved May 14, 2021, from CBC Radio: https://www.cbc.ca/radio/docproject/the-grader-operator-s-widow-1.4647084

Tolhurst, K., & Mordaunt, P. (2019, July 21). *Crack down on misuse of non-disclosure agreements in the workplace.* Retrieved May 14, 2021, from GOV.UK: https://www.gov.uk/government/news/crack-down-on-misuse-of-non-disclosure-agreements-in-the-workplace

Trask v Terra Nova Motors Ltd, 9836 (NL CA 1995). Retrieved May 14, 2021, from https://canlii.ca/t/2dxbg

Unger, D. (2020, September 11). *Union alleges "toxic workplace" for City of Winnipeg employees facing racism, bullying and harassment.* Retrieved May 14, 2021, from CTV News Winnipeg: https://winnipeg.ctvnews.ca/union-alleges-toxic-workplace-for-city-of-winnipeg-employees-facing-racism-bullying-and-harassment-1.5101895

Vigil highlights harassment, bullying at City of Edmonton. (2018, November 17). Retrieved May 11, 2021, from CBC Edmonton: https://www.cbc.ca/news/canada/edmonton/city-edmonton-employee-harassment-bullying-vigil-1.4910603

Vorvis v Insurance Corporation of British Columbia, 93 A SCR 1085 (SCC 1989). Retrieved May 14, 2021, from https://canlii.ca/t/1ft6t

Wallace v United Grain Growers Ltd. (2021, April 1). Retrieved May 11, 2021, from Wikipedia: https://en.wikipedia.org/wiki/Wallace_v_United_Grain_Growers_Ltd

Wallace v United Grain Growers Ltd., 332 3 SCR 701 (SCC 1997). Retrieved May 14, 2021, from https://canlii.ca/t/1fqxh,

What is discrimination? (2020, November 5). Retrieved May 11, 2021, from Canadian Human Rights Commission: https://www.chrc-ccdp.gc.ca/en/about-human-rights/what-discrimination

What is servant leadership? (2021). Retrieved May 14, 2021, from Robert L. Greenleaf Center for Servant Leadership: https://www.greenleaf.org/what-is-servant-leadership/

Whistleblowing. (n.d.). Retrieved May 14, 2021, from The Free Dictionary: https://legal-dictionary.thefreedictionary.com/Whistleblowing

Wilkie, D. (n.d.). *Workplace gossip: What crosses the line?* Retrieved May 11, 2021, from Society for Human Resources Management: Dana Wilkie, "Workplace Gossip: What Crosses the Line," Society for Human Resource Management (SHRM), https://www.shrm.org/resourcesandtools/hr-topics/employee-relations/pages/office-gossip-policies.aspx

Yamada, D. C. (2008). Workplace bullying and ethical leadership. *Journal of Values-Based Leadership, 1*(2), 49. Retrieved from https://scholar.valpo.edu/cgi/viewcontent.cgi?article=1032&context=jvbl

Printed in Canada